The Artful Traveller

The Flâneur's Guidebook

David Tuffley

To my beloved Nation of Four
Concordia Domi – Foris Pax

A good traveller has no fixed plans
and is not intent on arriving.
— Lao Tzu

Published 2013 by Altiora Publications
AltioraPublications.com

ISBN-13: 978-1463701765 ISBN-10: 1463701764

Cover Design by Double P Design Group: www.doublepdesign.com.au

About the Author

David Tuffley PhD is a Lecturer and researcher at Griffith University in Australia. David has a broad range of interests; Anthropology, Psychology, Philosophy, Ancient and Modern History, Linguistics, Rhetoric, Comparative Religions, Architectural History, Environments and Ecosystems.

Acknowledgements

So many to acknowledge; Lao Tzu, John St Clair, Steve Tuffley, Mark Twain, R.L. Stevenson, Samuel Johnson, Jack Kerouac, John Steinbeck, Aldous Huxley, D.H. Lawrence, Paul Theroux, Ralph Waldo Emerson, Robert Frost, Lao Tzu, T.S. Eliot, Anatol France, Seneca, Rudyard Kipling, G.K. Chesterton, St Augustine, and Ernest Hemingway for their ideas on the essence of travel. This book has been a work in progress since 1970.

Also the *Turrbal* and *Jagera* indigenous peoples, on whose ancestral land I write this book. This ancient continent has a profound story for those who would listen.

Contents

INTRODUCTION 6

    A WINNING DESIGN 7

    WHAT PEOPLE NEED 8

    LEAVING YOUR COMFORT ZONE 9

1. THE FLÂNEUR...11

    REDEFINING FLÂNEUR AS ARTFUL TRAVELLER 11

    BLENDING IN...13

    THE MOBILE FLÂNEUR..15

    GETTING LOST AND FINDING YOURSELF 16

    USING EMPATHY...19

    LEARNING THE LANGUAGE OF ARCHITECTURE...........................20

    TAKING PHOTOGRAPHS 22

2. PORTRAIT OF THE ARTFUL TRAVELLER........................23

    CHOOSING BETWEEN SAFETY AND RISK 24

    SEEING THE WORLD REALISTICALLY..25

    ACCEPTING THE WORLD AS IT IS 25

    BEING UNHAMPERED BY CONVENTION....................................26

    BEING AUTONOMOUS 27

    IMPROVING ONESELF CONTINUOUSLY.....................................27

    APPRECIATING THE WORLD ANEW 28

    ENJOYING SOLITUDE 28

    HAVING PEAK EXPERIENCES 29

3. BEING INTUITIVE...34

    MUNDANE INTUITION 35

    DEEP INTUITION..38

    CULTIVATING INTUITION 40

    SYNCHRONICITY 42

    COMMUNING WITH NATURE 43

4. BEING MINDFUL 48

Contents

PRACTICING MINDFULNESS 49
EXPERIENCING LIFE FULLY, VIVIDLY, SELFLESSLY 51
SEEING THE CHAIN OF CAUSE AND EFFECT 52
OVERCOMING PAST TRAUMA 53
JUDGING VERSUS UNDERSTANDING 54

5. BEING IN HARMONY WITH THE WORLD **56**

HARMONY WITH NATURE 58
KNOWING THE TAO 61
   What is the Tao? 61
   Alignment with the subtle 62
   Using what is not there 63
   The essence 63
   You do not have a life, you are life 63
   The origins of creativity 64
   Greatness 64
   An evolutionary force 65
   Polarity 65
   Proactive not reactive 66
   The ineffable cause 67
   The patterns of Nature 68
USING THE TAO TO BECOME MORE CONSCIOUS 68
   Sameness of bearing 69
   Being non-competitive 69
   Limiting sensual desire 70
   A true win-win situation 71
   Merge with the cycles of Nature 71
   Instincts and intuition 71
   Contemplating the subtle 72
   Influence without motive 73
   Avoiding extremes and full maturity 74
   The flame that burns twice as bright burns half as long 74
   Dwelling at the centre 75
   Envisaging a better world 76
   Oneness with the evolving universe 76
   The disease 77
USING THE TAO TO CULTIVATE ONESELF 78
   The pendulum of polarity 79
   Descending from the peak 79

Contents

Moderating the dynamic tension between polar opposites 80
Subtle influence 80
Independent perspective 81
Observing the patterns of Nature 82
Steady, incremental improvement 83
Mastery of self 83
Needing less 84
Keeping an open mind 85
Dwelling in the Tao 86
Remaining flexible and adaptable 86
The great leveller of extremes 87
Being magnanimous 89
Living for the maximum benefit of others 89
USING THE TAO TO LEAD OTHERS 90
The steady force of attitude 91
Subtle influence 92
Maintaining simplicity 92
Gravitas 94
Coordinating collective effort 95
Guide rather than rule 95
Cultivating one-ness 96
Unity of effort 96
Replace rigid rules with spontaneity 97
Like cooking a small fish 97
Uniting the group into a team 98
Avoid Machiavellian strategies 98
Humility 99
Compassion 99
USING THE TAO TO INFLUENCE GROUP DYNAMICS 99
Avoid self-aggrandisement 100
Avoid cunning and manipulation 101
Avoid aggression 101
Use force only when absolutely necessary 102
Cultivating restraint and humility 102
Knowing how much is enough 102
Avoiding escalation 103
Accepting blame 103
Promoting independence 104
USING THE TAO TO REFRAIN FROM ACTION 104

Contents

Selflessness.. *104*

Harmony.. *105*

Avoid becoming too specialised......................... *105*

Subtle influence... *106*

Strategic non-action.................................... *106*

Truth in non-action..................................... *107*

Being non-confrontational.............................. *107*

Like a river finding its way through a valley of boulders........... *108*

Recognising the beginning.............................. *109*

Give me freedom or give me death....................... *109*

The doomed leader...................................... *109*

6. COMMUNING WITH NATURE...................................... **111**

FELT-CONNECTEDNESS WITH ALL THINGS............................ 112

PRACTICE MINDFULNESS.. 113

RELAX AND MERGE.. 114

UNCONDITIONAL LOVE AND COMPASSION........................... 115

SOURCE AWARENESS... 115

7. BEING RATIONAL.. **117**

RATIONALITY & SCIENCE....................................... 118

ON THE NATURE OF EVIL....................................... 119

EVOLUTIONARY PSYCHOLOGY..................................... 121

SEVEN DEADLY SINS.. 123

UNDERSTANDING... 125

ETHNOCENTRIC THINKING...................................... 126

8. AIRLINE ETIQUETTE... **128**

THE PSYCHOLOGY OF AIRLINE TRAVEL............................ 128

Claustrophobia.. *129*

Personal space (Proxemics).............................. *129*

An attitude of gratitude................................ *130*

BEFORE THE FLIGHT.. 131

Patience... *131*

Consideration.. *131*

It's a cell phone not a megaphone....................... *132*

DURING THE FLIGHT.. 133

Contain yourself in your allocated space................ *133*

The battle for the armrest.............................. *133*

Contents

The rapid recliner 134
Under your seat 135
Getting up 136
The window shade 137
Moderate how much alcohol you consume 137
Kicking children, screaming babies 138
Follow the flight attendant's directives 139
The talkative passenger 140
The mile-high club 140
Personal hygiene 141
AFTER THE FLIGHT 141
Stay seated until it is possible to disembark 141
Double check you have the right bag 141

APPENDIX A: MEDITATION MADE SIMPLE **143**

SIMPLE METHOD FOR MEDITATION 144
PRACTICE NON-ATTACHMENT 147
OPTIONAL MANTRA 148

APPENDIX B: ABOUT CAMERAS **149**

Introduction

We shall never cease from exploration,
and the end of all our exploring,
will be to arrive where we started,
and know the place for the first time - T.S. Eliot.

Travel is an expression of the human instinct for *freedom* and it is an instinct we share with every other creature on this planet. We all instinctively need freedom so we can move about and find what we need in life.

For many people living in the world today, travel is a luxury afforded once or twice a year, if at all. Living sedentary, indebted lives that keep us tethered to one place, the instinct to travel is frustrated but not extinguished.

When we do manage to get away, do we really enjoy the experience? Not if we approach it with the wrong mind-set. The same journey can be a source of pleasure or misery depending on your mind-set. When travel is done with an open mind, it can be a transformative experience. When approached with a rigid, judgmental mind, every encounter is unpleasant.

The Artful Traveller is a handbook for people everywhere wishing to deepen their appreciation of the art of travelling. Chances are, if you are reading this, you are such a person.

Read this book with an open mind. Suspend judgment long enough to absorb the message, then decide.

A winning design

What a spectacular species we humans are. There are many reasons why we have been so successful, what David Attenborough called our *'winning design'*; there is our adaptability, our tool-making and use of fire, our empathy and team-work, our creative imaginations, our search for improved ways of doing things, our ability to eat almost anything and adapt to almost any environment, and our ability to communicate. These are just some of the reasons. This book discusses an important but not well-understood aspect of our winning design, *the instinct to travel*.

The instinct to travel has led us colonise the entire planet. In the past 100,000 years this desire has taken us out of Africa to almost every habitat on earth, from the Polar Regions to the equatorial jungles. We will continue our expansion out into space with settlements on both the Moon and Mars well before the end of the 21st Century.

This is a remarkable achievement for a species that only 100,000 years ago, a blink of the eye in evolutionary terms, were hunter gathers doing their best to survive on the African savannah.

In the past, travelling, or roaming about was about survival. While early humans would have enjoyed looking at a beautiful landscape, for them it was primarily about finding food and shelter so they might live long enough to reproduce. With life expectancies in the 20's, life in those days was indeed *nasty, short and brutish*.

What people need

Today, in the developed world most of the problems of survival have been solved. People live mostly sedentary lives where their needs are met by an abundance of consumer goods and services. Yet stroll about the city streets or shopping malls and look objectively at people. Notice how few seem happy despite the abundance that surrounds them? Most walk about with a blank expression, some look downright unhappy.

People do not just have needs; they have a *hierarchy* of needs. While people's lower order needs might be met, if their higher order needs for a meaningful life, for self-esteem and self-actualisation are *not* met, they will be unhappy.

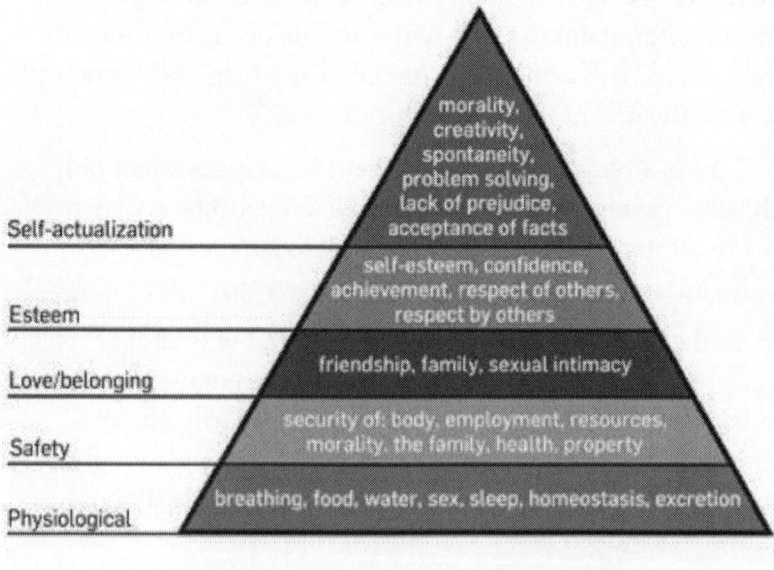

Figure 1: Maslow's Hierarchy of Human Needs.

The psychologist Abraham Maslow describes this phenomenon in his *Hierarchy of Human Needs* model. To be happy, Maslow held that people need to satisfy the lower-order needs for food, shelter, sex, then the middle-order needs for safety and security, then the higher middle-order needs for love and belonging. Above these is the higher-order need for self-esteem. But the highest need of all, sitting like the capstone on a pyramid is *Self-Actualisation*.

The Artful Traveller, the person described in this book, is someone who has progressively learned how to satisfy their lower and middle order needs, and who now realises that travel is one route towards self-actualisation.

Leaving your comfort zone

Travelling is a brutality. It forces you to trust strangers and to lose sight of all that familiar comfort of home and friends. You are constantly off balance. Nothing is yours except the essential things – air, sleep, dreams, the sea, the sky – all things tending towards the eternal or what we imagine of it. – Cesare Pavese.

Travelling *should* take you out of your comfort zone.

It is understandable that people want to feel safe and comfortable, but insisting on feeling this way when travelling is unrealistic.

Think of the stereotypical traveller abroad who leaves us in no doubt as to where they are from as they loudly proclaim their nationality, often in a way that causes offence to those who witness it. They do this because they are uncomfortable being out of their native culture which up until then they had taken for granted, much the same way that fish takes water for granted. Their priority is to re-create their comfort zone by engulfing themselves in a bubble of familiar noise.

Not only do they engender contempt with this behaviour, they have isolated themselves from experiencing the place they are in. If they experience anything, it is the negative reaction of the local people. They might as well have stayed home.

The Art of Travel has much to do with finding a way to transcend our instinctive need to belong to a tribe or group. This instinct leads us to categorise the world in terms of 'us good, them bad'. Tribalism must be replaced by an open mind that does not judge and compare.

This is not an easy thing to do. Our species has survived for millions of years by bonding tightly in family groups (us) and by default regarding everyone else (them) as potential enemies. But there is no place in today's connected world for this primitive attitude. We are all one big human family now.

1. The Flâneur

The *Flâneur* (or *Flâneuse* in the feminine) is an idea originating with the French poet Charles Baudelaire. In Baudelaire's world, the Flâneur was an idly-rich dandy, who wandered the streets of 19th century Paris seeking a remedy for ever-threatening ennui.

In this book, the 19th century Flâneur is re-born in the 21st century as *the Artful Traveller; someone, not necessarily wealthy or idle, who seeks an authentic experience of a city by strolling about in an unstructured way, responding intuitively to what they encounter. The Artful Traveller remains detached, non-judgmental; appreciating the nuanced perceptions that come their way.*

Some readers might prefer to keep the old name, but since the original concept of the Flâneur has been re-defined and expanded, a new name is needed to distinguish it from the old - the *Artful Traveller*.

Redefining Flâneur as Artful Traveller

The Artful Traveller, in common with the Flâneur, sets out with a beginning and possibly an end in mind; but what happens in between depends on the subtle aesthetic contours of the architecture and geography of the place in which they find themselves. The description that follows uses Paris as an example, in recognition of the origins of the Artful Traveller, but it applies equally to any city or town, anywhere in the world.

The Artful Traveller has no interest in joining the long queue for the Eifel Tower. Five hours, what a waste of time! Instead they find the road less-travelled, the backstreets. As they stroll, they feel the ambience, hear the conversations, notice the architecture and the way people inhabit it, smell the coffee and lunch cooking, marvel at the quality of the light and notice how the moss grows in the cracks between the paving stones. All of this and much more.

The Artful Traveller's senses are wide open. In no hurry, they are fully alive and absorbed in the world around them. They do not wish to be anywhere else. They have taken to heart Lao Tzu's advice that *a good traveller has no fixed plans and is not intent on arriving.*

The Artful Traveller goes about with an air of appreciation and respect. This will be reflected in their body language, and the locals will instinctively respond well to it. They treat beggars with compassion, perhaps giving them a small sum of money and always a kind word.

Soon, the vividly perceived impressions of the place assemble in the mind of the traveller into a richly textured montage. When this reaches a critical mass, their imagination shifts into overdrive; what happens next might be described as a peak experience.

If the Artful Traveller wishes to experience the view from the top of the Eifel Tower, they will probably have noticed that there is no queue for the stairs that goes up to the half-way point. A small sign says that from there they can take an elevator to the top. Strolling past the people waiting in the long queue, they begin the climb. It is an arduous but authentic experience, a chance to look at the unfolding city and to feel as though they have earned the view from the top.

The Artful Traveller experience is the antithesis of the organised tour. It is true that a package tour is sometimes the sensible option; perhaps time is limited, or it is unsafe to walk about unaccompanied. If possible though, the Artful Traveller avoids being herded about. They know that this insulates them from having an authentic experience of the place.

The Artful Traveller's goal is to encounter new and authentic experiences through intuitively-directed drifting. The process has been described by Guy Debord as *a mode of experimental behaviour linked to the conditions of urban society: a technique of rapid passage through varied ambiances.*

Blending in

The Artful Traveller moves through a cityscape almost invisibly because they blend in. The aim is to appear like a local, or at least not a foreigner.

The principle is the same as blending into the natural environment so that the creatures that live there are not alarmed by your presence. Have you noticed how the forest goes quiet when you enter it? But if you sit in silence for a few minutes, the forest comes back to life. The creatures resume what they were doing before you arrived. They are aware of your presence, but are not threatened by you now.

To blend in, one dresses and moves about much as a local person might. If you are carrying map, conceal it inside a folded newspaper. Learn a few basic expressions in the local language. Try to communicate with people in that language.

You know it is working when strangers approach you, asking for directions. Once I was in the French city of Metz, exploring the old part of town near the cathedral where the bones of William the Conqueror lay for centuries. I was leaning against a post on a street corner enjoying the ambience when a Frenchman in a Renault pulled up beside me and asked me for directions. I gave a Gallic shrug and said *désolé, je suis un étranger ici* (sorry, I'm a stranger here).

Figure 2: Cathédrale Saint Etienne de Metz.

I had just read the inscription of a nearby monument and was reflecting on it. I learned that the town is very old, going back to Roman times. In the 1,800 years since the Romans left, Metz has passed many times back and forth between what we now call France and Germany. I realised that Metz is now and forever a French city. Since the end of World War II and the establishment of the European Union, France and Germany are now economically dependent on each other which effectively stops them from ever going to war again. This must have been the thinking behind the EU. No more war. In the spirit of enlightened self-interest, you do not wage war against a country if it will harm your own interests.

By taking a leisurely stroll around the old town, and stopping to read and think about what this place meant, I had a series of authentic experiences that I will never forget and which I would have missed had I made a structured itinerary and timetable for myself. Indeed, I probably would not have gone to Metz at all if high profile tourist attractions were my priority. One can still visit big attractions, woven into the fabric of the day.

The mobile Flâneur

While the Flâneur was always on foot, the modern day Artful Traveller might be on foot or mobile, the same principles apply. If mobile, they drive or ride about in the same unstructured way, responding moment-by-moment and in a non-judgmental way to what they encounter. It is the nuances they seek, and these can only be noticed and appreciated when one is unhurried and open-minded.

The advantage to the Artful Traveller of being mobile is obvious enough; one can cover a lot more ground this way, and do so in comfort and safety. The disadvantage is that it is easy to miss the subtle nuances of a place if one is cocooned in a vehicle, particularly when you have a destination in mind. For this reason, driving in cities or on high-speed motorways should be avoided unless your primary purpose is to get somewhere fast, perhaps to make a travel connection. The Artful Traveller prefers to experience a city on foot, with public transport as a backup.

When in the countryside, the Artful Traveller takes the road less travelled, the quiet country lanes and by-ways used by the local residents. On these it will not matter if you slow down or stop altogether to look at something interesting.

Bicycles offer an almost ideal compromise between extending your range in cities and the countryside while being able to move about in a very leisurely manner. Motor bikes and scooters are the most fun of all, but also the most dangerous.

GPS navigators are an essential item, but the virtue of a GPS can also be a vice. They remove the need to look at a map as you drive, but their incessant commands become annoying. The Artful Traveller mutes the sound, but keeps it switched on and ready to get to work.

Getting lost and finding yourself

Getting lost can be a blessing *and* a curse for the Artful Traveller. All kinds of interesting and spontaneous experiences can happen, but you can also find that you are *so* lost that you have not a clue where you are, and no easy way

of finding out. Where you draw that line between blessing
and curse depends on your personal tolerance towards
uncertainty.

Paradoxically, getting lost can be a way of finding yourself
in the sense that you discover something about yourself that
you would not find as long as you stay in your comfort zone.
There is no need to plan for these experiences; they have a
way of finding *you*. Life has a way of giving you the
experiences you need, not necessarily the one's you want.

For example, once I was in Berlin. The year was 2002, and I
had returned after being part of the momentous events of
November 1989 (when the Wall came down). Naturally I
wanted to see what had changed during 13 years of re-
unification. Berlin is a sprawling city, so I hired a car, the
better to explore this fascinating city.

Many Berlin districts were in the process of urban renewal
following re-unification, but some looked curiously thread-
bare. Walking around one of these, I found myself in a
microcosm of old East Germany, formerly known as the
Deutsche Demokratische Republik or DDR. From the shops
selling communist era food, like the baker with *DDR
Broetchen* (East German Rolls), the tobacconist selling East
German cigarettes like *f6* brand, and the Trabant cars parked
at the kerb it was clear that nostalgia for the old days existed
here. I learned later that this phenomenon is called *ostalgie* in
German (nostalgia for the East) and was common throughout
the former DDR at that time.

Despite the lack of consumer goods, many East Germans
had been happy under the old system. This attitude had
become embedded in the culture and was not to be as easily

as exchanging a Trabant for a Golf. It became clear to me as I
strolled about that the ideological struggle between
Capitalism and Communism was not as black and white as it
is sometimes represented. The situation was a more complex
and nuanced struggle. I reflected on this as ate a lunch of
DDR-style *kartoffeln (mashed potatoes) mit sauerkraut,* and
enjoyed its simple goodness.

It was time to return to the hotel, but frustratingly I could
not orient myself on the map. I had wandered so far, for so
long in the labyrinth of old East Berlin that I was completely
disoriented. Few people understood English, and I was
unable to make myself understood in German. A GPS would
have solved this problem, but these were rare in hire cars in
2002.

I did however know where the car was parked. So for the
next three hours I drove around looking for landmarks
without success. I was becoming desperate. It seemed the
best thing to do was to park the car in a safe place, catch a
taxi to the hotel, and let the hire car company come and get
the car for a fee. How embarrassing.

When I finally stopped resisting the reality of the situation
and feeling sorry for myself, I began to see things more
clearly. It occurred to me that the setting sun was an
important clue; which way was West. Knowing that the hotel
was in the former West Berlin, I reasoned that if I drove in
that direction, I might just find the Kurfürstendamm and the
hotel. Half an hour later, guided only by the setting sun, the
hotel came into view. What a wonderful sight!

Getting lost was stressful, but the experience was a good
one to add to the Artful Traveller repertoire. I had not only

experienced an authentic slice of East German life, far from the milling crowd at the Brandenburg Gate, I also learned something never to be forgotten about making contingency plans and following one's instincts to travel towards the setting sun.

Using empathy

Empathy is part of what makes human beings so spectacularly successful at working together in teams and living together in communities. Empathy is possible because in our brains are nerve cells called *mirror neurons*. These allow us to experience, by proxy, what another person is experiencing; to develop what psychologists call a *theory of mind* about what another person is thinking.

Empathy can remind us how much we have in common with people. By empathising with the people we encounter in our travels, it becomes clear that culture is but a thin veneer that creates the appearance of difference, but that just beneath the surface is a person just like us. It allows us to see all humanity as one big extended family.

The Artful Traveller uses empathy to build a bridge of understanding with people. When you are empathic, the people you encounter sense this understanding in your demeanour and will generally react favourably to it.

For example, once I was in Monterey, California, on my way from a work event in Portland to another in San Diego. I stayed several days in Monterey because it is so beautiful, and also to experience what might have inspired John Steinbeck, Henry Miller and Robert Louis Stevenson.

I was strolling around the waterfront and found myself near the Monterey Bay Coast Guard Station. Just cruising around, looking at the boats, enjoying the ambience. As I looked out to sea, it occurred to me that my wife and children, who I missed, were all the way on the other side of this wide Pacific Ocean. I felt both connected to them and separated from them by the ocean.

As I was experiencing this, a woman with two young children walked past me. As they passed I heard the younger ask plaintively; *Mom, when is Daddy coming home?* There was a perfect symmetry to that moment. Empathy helped me to realize that this family was like mine on the other side of the ocean, all of us feeling the same way.

Learning the language of architecture

The Artful Traveller deepens their experience of a place by learning the language of architecture. Every building is making an on-going statement to the world. It communicates the values of the person or institution that built it. For example, a wealthy man may build himself a grand house which says to the world, *I am rich and powerful*. The grand country houses of the British and European aristocracy of the past are all making such a statement. Even more so we see King Louis XIV of France who built perhaps the grandest palace of all in Versailles. Its purpose was to house the Royal Court, but equally important, it was to impress visitors with

King Louis' wealth and power. It was a foolish nobleman anywhere who built a bigger palace than the King himself had.

Baroque architecture is seen all over Europe in Cathedrals and Palaces and public buildings. This architectural form was an attempt to win back support for Roman Catholicism during the Reformation when Matin Luther and the various Protestant movements across Europe saw many people leave the established church. Baroque was intended to be a glimpse of heaven, a promise to the faithful of what awaited them in the next life. The austere, unadorned Protestant churches interiors offered no such glimpse of paradise. Even today, the splendour of some Baroque edifices is still truly breath-taking to the modern eye accustomed to wonders. Imagine how impressive it must have been several hundred years ago.

Visit any city that was once an imperial capital (London, Paris, Rome, Madrid, St Petersburg) and you will see many buildings that still express the power and majesty of an empire that has now passed into history.

Learning the language of architecture allows you to look at buildings and be able to interpret the non-verbal statement they are making. It can enrich the travel experience greatly. When you visit a new city, you can wander about and read the story that its buildings tell. It is usually a dramatic story that you would otherwise not get to hear.

Taking photographs

Taking photographs of the many interesting things they see in their travels is an indispensable part of the whole Artful Traveller experience for many of those who practice it. It is not essential though. Operating a camera can be a technical challenge that gets in the way of one's aesthetic enjoyment of a place.

Photography is a mode of artistic expression that lends itself well to the practice of Artful Travel. It goes beyond the cataloguing of worthy sights to the creation of meaningful artefacts that tell a larger story than a simple catalogue of photos. The best of these photos thus created can be assembled into a narrative that goes some way towards capturing the subjective experiences of the day.

Travel photography is a large topic, well beyond the scope of this book. This section simply introduces the topic. It is understood that many readers will already be accomplished photographers. Those who are not and would like to be can consult the wealth of published material on the topic.

For reference, Appendix B has more information on cameras.

2. Portrait of the Artful Traveller

You are not only a unique person today, there is also a *potential you* to be realised in the future. That person is the fullest expression of your essential humanity. That person is amazing.

The fully-realised you is capable of great achievements. Whatever you are doing with your life, you should be making it your priority to realise this future self. You could say that it is your purpose in being alive. Can you think of a better mission in life?

Since everyone is unique, there is no *one* way for a person to become self-actualized. Beware of those who say there is one (right) way. The best way is to find your *own* way. But how? By being shown a portrait, then using your imagination to find a way to morph yourself into your own unique version of that portrait. Doing this will not compromise who you are, it will *intensify* who you are.

Self-actualised people do more than travel, they have fuller lives and being self-actualised informs every part of their life. Being an Artful Traveller is a sub-set, a microcosm of the fuller self, but there is no reason why you cannot become self-actualised through cultivating your inner Artful Traveller. Yes, this book can be a path towards the greater goal of self-actualisation.

Choosing between safety and risk

To awaken quite alone in a strange town is one of the pleasantest sensations in the world. – Freya Stark.

Life is a moment-by-moment choice between safety (out of fear and need for defence) and risk (for the sake of progress and growth): The Artful Traveller consciously makes the growth choice as often as they can.

Observe your own mind in action. You will notice that this continuum (with safety at one end and risk at the other) is often active in your thinking.

There is a dynamic tension between these two opposites, and through habit you will lean towards one or the other. If you are like many people, you are probably inclined towards the safe, low-risk option because you want predictability with no unpleasant surprises.

The Artful Traveller may still value comfort and security, but they know that personal growth is slow while they are in their comfort-zone. They therefore take themselves out of their comfort zone as often as they can to create the right conditions for interesting experiences to occur.

The essence of being an Artful Traveller is summed up in this quote from The Buddha:

But if you do not find an intelligent companion, a wise and well-behaved person going the same way as yourself, then go on your way alone, like a king abandoning a conquered kingdom, or like a great elephant in the deep forest – The Buddha.

Seeing the world realistically

The Artful Traveller sees the world realistically, rigorously avoiding delusion or wishful thinking. They usually have a superior ability to reason, to see the truth even when it is more comfortable not to.

The Artful Traveller is unthreatened by the unknown. They know that fear of the unknown can paralyse a person into staying inside their comfort zone where they are unlikely to experience anything new.

Their realistic outlook enables them to avoid real and present danger, thus allowing them to have experiences that others might think are too risky.

Accepting the world as it is

The Artful Traveller accepts the world as it is without wishing it to be otherwise. They manage their expectations, and accept themselves, other people and the world at large, knowing that to do otherwise leads to frustration.

Accepting the world as it is does not mean resigning oneself to a bad situation. You can still take action to remedy a situation. Acceptance simply means that while you are in the process of extracting yourself from a situation, you are not resisting the reality of it by thinking *'this should not be happening'*. The Artful Traveller deals with it without complaining.

25

The Artful Traveller has rid themselves of crippling guilt knowing that this emotion has a strongly corrosive effect on their enjoyment of life. They know that everyone makes mistakes. They do not waste their time and energy feeling guilty; they make amends, resolve to not do it again, and move forwards with a clear conscience.

The Artful Traveller is able to enjoy themselves without regret, having been released from *unnecessary* inhibitions.

Being unhampered by convention

The Artful Traveller is unhampered by convention or orthodox views on how people or the world should be. They know that Orthodoxy can be a strait-jacket for the imagination. It constrains creativity and limits spontaneity. But they do not flaunt their unorthodox views in ways that are likely to annoy others. Why create conflict unless it is absolutely necessary?

Their accurate perception of reality allows them to base their actions on evolving reality, not on orthodox thinking. Therefore they see the world as it is, not as others believe it should be

Being unconventional is not without cost. The person who moves out of the orthodoxy is likely to be punished by the group for their non-conformist thinking as a way to bring them back into the fold where it is comfortable. The Artful Traveller is not prepared to trade their freedom for this security.

Being autonomous

The Artful Traveller have internalised their own well-considered ethical standards. They do not being told how to act by an external source. They have the integrity to live by these standards even under extreme pressure. For example if they find themselves in a situation where mass hysteria has taken hold.

They have a robust resilience in the face of inevitable set-backs and hard-knocks.

The Artful Traveller keeps a degree of self-contained independence from the good and bad opinion of others. Guided by their own principles they understand that reward and punishment is how people and society controls our behaviour, so they are able to resist attempts to manipulate them.

Improving oneself continuously

The Artful Traveller knows that in an evolving world the time-honoured ways of doing things may no longer be the best way. They look realistically at a situation and on the merits of the situation decide on the best way to handle it.

They are not usually content to 'leave well enough alone', or to subscribe to the *'if it ain't broke don't fix it'* view. They know that not every improvement they make will work as hoped, and that failure is often the price of success.

Appreciating the world anew

The Artful Traveller has a fresh rather than stereotyped appreciation of people and places, giving them a new perspective on every situation they encounter.

They avoid making judgements and comparisons between the world they are experiencing and the world from which they came. In simple terms, they live in the now.

The Artful Traveller knows that moment-to-moment living is thrilling, transcendent and spiritual.

Enjoying solitude

Feeling the need to deeply consider their experiences, the Artful Traveller has a greater than average need for privacy. While the company of people can be enjoyed, too much company can unduly influence one. The Artful Traveller therefore tends to be more detached than most.

Alone but not lonely, the Artful Traveller experiences the world vividly and directly. They retain their dignity even when there is confusion around them, when people are hysterical and blaming. They are resilient in the face of set-backs. They refuse to feel like a victim. This emotional independence allows the Artful Traveller to go where and when they want to go, doing what they want to do. They are in charge of their own destiny, taking responsibly for their successes and failures. Nobel Laureate (1907) Rudyard

Kipling sums it up thus in his classic poem *If--*, written in 1895:

> *If you can keep your head when all about you*
> *Are losing theirs and blaming it on you;*
> *If you can trust yourself when all men doubt you,*
> *But make allowance for their doubting too;*
> *If you can wait and not be tired by waiting,*
> *Or, being lied about, don't deal in lies,*
> *Or, being hated, don't give way to hating,*
> *And yet don't look too good, nor talk too wise;*

Having peak experiences

Peak experiences are how you know you have become a fully-fledged Artful Traveller. They become your most treasured memories, never to be forgotten.

Cultivating a mind-set characterised by the attitudes discussed above may not produce peak experiences on demand, but such a mind-set will make it far more likely that they will occur spontaneously, often when least expected. It has happened this way with me many times. It could be driving through the Tuscan countryside, or along the Pacific Coast Highway at Big Sur, or sitting on a bed of moss in a New Zealand rain forest when everything comes together and the experience of being merged completely with the world around me comes. I call this a Satori moment, after the Zen way of describing such things. It has also been called a peak experience by Maslow.

The phenomenon of *peak experience* or *flow* has been described by Maslow this way; *Feelings of limitless horizons opening up to the vision, the feeling of being simultaneously more powerful and also more helpless than one ever was before, the feeling of ecstasy and wonder and awe, the loss of placement in time and space with, finally, the conviction that something extremely important and valuable had happened, so that the subject was to some extent transformed and strengthened even in his daily life by such experiences. When peak experiences are especially powerful, the sense of self dissolves into an awareness of a greater unity.* (from Religion, Values and Peak Experiences, 1970).

Here is an example of a Peak Experience from my own life.

In keeping with the spirit of this book, I resolved to notice and appreciate the many small things around me as I went about my everyday life. To most people, these small things seem so ordinary, so common-place that they are easy to overlook, even scorn. Why then are these things worthy of our attention? It is because in their way, they are perfection. They have much to tell us if we stop and notice with a child's open mind. Everyday objects have something of great value to give if you would take a moment to receive it.

With this mind-set, one day I noticed the humble moss plants growing in the cracks between the paving stones as I walked from the car-park to my office at Griffith University's Nathan campus. This campus is set in the middle of a 1600 acre eucalyptus forest reserve in Brisbane. Moss is a common sight in shady places here where the dew lingers.

Moss is easy to overlook because we are often pre-occupied and it is so small and common. It is just one of thousands of objects passing through our visual field any day of our life. Choose one instance of this humble plant and look more closely. With a macro lens on my camera it was revealed as a beautiful forest, as lovely as any full-sized forest I had ever flown-over.

There is something quite beautiful about moss when seen up close, this perfectly adapted survivor on our planet for the past 500 million years. Getting down on my hands and knees to see more clearly made me feel humble. It was mind-expanding to think that this humble little plant had existed in its current form for so long. I tried to stretch my imagination across such a vast span of time.

Figure 3: Moss as a forest microcosm.

Having stretched my imagination so far into the past, I now tried sending it into the future by the same amount. Now I had a billion year span balanced on the fulcrum of the present moment. This modest little plant turned out to have a big story to tell.

The story it told me in that moment was that my appreciation of it was the *dream of the Earth realised*. Life seems to want to become conscious of its own existence. After four billion years of evolution, life on this planet had become aware of itself; a major achievement which I felt greatly privileged to be a part of. I knew, though, that the moss would have told the same story to anyone else willing to listen.

Unlike the moss, we humans will not survive a billion years in our current form. And when our species has morphed into something else or become extinct, the moss will still be modestly growing in shady places.

This train of thought, I realised, was a continuation of one which began 35 years earlier. In 1975 I visited an ancient forest in New Zealand. It was near the Southland town of Te Anau. The glaciated landscape is like that of the Cadillac National Park in Maine, or the fjord lands of Norway.

The forest here is as it has been since the last Ice Age, perhaps 8,000 years, though this kind of forest had probably grown here on and off for many millions of years before that during the inter-glacial periods.

The trees were magnificent; tall, straight, and majestic. There was a quality to the light filtering through the forest canopy that gave this place a transcendent beauty. It was like something out of Tolkein's *Lord of the Rings*.

Figure 4: Moss as a forest macrocosm near Te Anau, NZ.

The moss in this rain forest covered every bit of available ground with a layer perhaps half a meter thick or more in places. It was soft underfoot, like walking on a mattress. It exhaled a sweet earthy breath when I walked on it. An immense reverence for that moss swept through me. I wanted to sink into it, be embraced by it, become one with it.

In that peak-experience, as I lay on the moss, something in me resonated with and became one with the spirit of the forest. It was a moment of complete enchantment, of self-actualisation. As Maslow describes; *the feeling of ecstasy and wonder and awe, the loss of placement in time and space with, finally, the conviction that something extremely important and valuable had happened ... when peak experiences are especially powerful, the sense of self dissolves into an awareness of a greater unity.*

3. Being intuitive

The word *intuition* is from the Latin *intueri*, meaning 'to look inside' or 'to contemplate'. It is usually defined in dictionaries as being able to understand something immediately, without the need for rational thought. It is a knowing that comes from a person's sub-conscious mind.

Arising from the sub-conscious, intuition comes naturally to people, yet the clear perception of it can be clouded by having a conscious mind that is too busy, loud or chaotic to clearly perceive it. When used in conjunction with the rational mind, they make an unbeatable team that lets you clearly perceive your best course of action in a given situation. It is all about balancing the mostly logical left brain with the largely intuitive right-brain.

In the developed world, it is common for people to be heavily skewed towards left-brain use. Some of us need to re-learn how to more fully use the right-brain. We were born with this ability, but is suppressed by an education system that values hard, empirical facts over imagination.

This chapter explores the nature of intuition and shows you how to cultivate it as a valuable adjunct to your rational mind. It also discusses how the Artful Traveller might use it to good effect to enhance their travel experience.

Mundane intuition

In our evolutionary past, ordinary intuition developed as a survival mechanism; a pattern matching capability that compared what a person perceived moment by moment with what had been experienced in the past. Experiences are remembered as a pattern. When the pattern of the perceptual field of the current experience matches a remembered pattern, we experience intuition. If there are implications of danger, you have a hunch to get ready for fight or flight. In advantageous situations, like the presence of food, the instinct is to investigate more closely.

An example in the modern world is the case of speed cameras. In Australia, law enforcement agencies use ordinary-looking white vans parked on busy roads to photograph speeding vehicles at random locations. When driving one day, I noticed a parked white van several hundred meters ahead. A sense of unease quickly came over me, less than a second after noticing the van. My first impulse was to check my speed. I had simply recognised a remembered and matched a pattern that represented danger; in this case the danger of being fined and acquiring demerit points on my driver's license.

Extending this principle to commonly encountered situations, intuition is an invaluable part of being an Artful Traveller. Some might even call it *common sense*. When strolling about a foreign city, for example, it will help you to recognise the indications of an unsafe area.

Intuition helps you to get a general sense for a situation, and then logic can be used to validate the intuition. A good analogy for how to do this comes from software engineering. It must be stressed that this is an analogy. New software is tested in two stages to make sure it both conforms to the requirements specification *and* that it does what it is supposed to do in world. In other words, it is tested in the development environment, and then tested again in the user environment. The process is called *Verification and Validation* (V&V). These two words might sound synonymous, but they have distinctly different meanings in this context. *Verification* means checking correctness in the development environment, and *Validation* is ensuring correctness in the real-world.

To apply the analogy, your intuition makes a suggestion which you quickly *verify* with your rational mind in case (a) the recognised pattern is different from the one you remember, or (b) it is the same pattern but you have drawn the wrong conclusion from it. It is important not to over-think this part. Your first impression is usually the correct one.

The second stage, validation, is done when you use your rational mind to decide what to do, and as you are doing it, *validate* that this course of action is working, and fine tune it in the light of new information. V&V makes a good team and will rarely if ever lead you astray.

High-achieving people across many fields of endeavour report that their creative process proceeds in this way. An idea emerges from their intuitive right-brain, and then they use their rational left-brain to work out the details of how to make it happen. They are making full and proper use of the cognitive resources available on both sides of their brain.

The preceding could be described as ordinary intuition. But there is also a deeper, more mysterious level of intuition available to those who would cultivate it. The process is the same as for mundane intuition, but the insight is coming from a deeper source, not a previously remembered experience. Typically, one learns more in a single flash of such insight than can be learned from an external source in days or weeks. This is the *Ah Ha!* or *Eureka* moment. Artists call it inspiration. Maslow would call it a *peak experience*. But the label we put on it does not matter, the label is not the phenomenon, just a name. What matters is how it can be cultivated so that we, as Artful Travellers, can create the right conditions for it to occur spontaneously.

The hard-core rationalist will likely reject this whole idea since a way has not yet been found to test it objectively, empirically. And yet, inspiration, or deep intuition as I call it in this book, has been experienced by an assortment of thinkers from diverse cultures and historical periods. Stroll around Renaissance Florence and marvel at the fruits of deep intuition.

Hard-core rationalists believe that unless something can be objectively tested, it does not exist in any real sense. The Artful Traveller keeps an open mind, intuitively understanding that there is far more to the world than is currently understood by science. As Hamlet said *there are more things in heaven and earth, Horatio, than are dreamt of in your philosophy.*

Deep intuition

To understand intuition at a deeper level, it is necessary to be familiar with the concept of *Microcosm-Macrocosm*. A review of religions and mystical traditions reveals it as a recurring theme. Indeed, it appears so frequently in schools of thought that are independent of each other that it might even be described as a universal human truth, having been independently recognised by astute observers from different backgrounds and historical periods.

The idea of *Microcosm-Macrocosm* is expressed in different terms in various religions and philosophies, according to the culture of the times, but the underlying idea remains the same. For example, in Hinduism is the *Brahman-Atman* linkage. Within each of us is the *Atman*, our essential self that is beyond the world of form, and *Brahmin* the universal spirit from which the world of form arises. Brahmin and Atman are qualitatively the same, though differing in scale. The only way a person can know Brahmin is through knowing their Atman. In Christianity is mention of the God Within.

The idea is that the inner you is a scaled-down, perfectly formed copy of the outer universe. Like a raindrop falling into a lake. It is all water, though the scales of magnitude differ. It is tremendously liberating and empowering to realise that everything that exists in the universe also exists, in a representative way at least, within you. Any knowledge you have of the outer universe comes through the corresponding component within you.

The ancient Greeks believed that only by knowing this microcosm can a person know the macrocosm. A person cannot know the macrocosm directly, only by knowing the microcosm, one's inner self, then generalising to the macrocosm. They summed it up as *Know Thyself*, as inscribed above the door in the forecourt of the Temple of Apollo in Delphi.

Figure 5: Gnothi Sauton (Know Thyself).

Artists, philosophers, scientists, people whose thoughts change the world with the creative power of their ideas have found a way to know themselves, their microcosmic self, and to bring that awareness into the material world of form. They know it as the well-spring of their creativity. Ideas coming from this sacred inner space are communicated to the conscious mind of the artist by intuition and from there it is conveyed into the world where others delight to see it, perhaps recognising its origins as non-mundane.

The Artful Traveller likewise works to know themselves and access the wealth of intuitive knowledge that exists, has always existed within themselves. They bring it into their daily awareness and use it to enrich their lives.

Cultivating intuition

Intuition can be cultivated by building an awareness that your microcosmic inner self is a small but perfectly formed representation of the macrocosm outside. It is how you are connected to all things; in a sense you *are* all things. The felt awareness of this truth is enlightenment according to some mystical traditions. You don't just think it, you *feel* that it is true, know it at a deep level.

You no longer identify with the world of form as your *primary* reality. You identify instead with your inner reality, while the outside world is your secondary reality. You continue to recognise the world of form as a relative truth so that you are able to function within it and be effective, but it is no longer your primary reality.

Most people in the world do not think this way; they think the outside world is primary, and give scant regard to their inner reality, thus contributing through neglect to the chaos of their lives.

So intuition is the bridge between the world of form and the formless realm of ideas that lies beyond it.

The Artful Traveller, as they go about in the world, consciously recognises the world as an interconnected system that relates to a scaled-down version within themselves. *I am the world and the world is me.* They do *not* see the outside world as a big chaotic assembly of unconnected parts, and they separate from it. They look for the connections that exist behind the appearance of separateness. As they make progress in seeing the connections, they will increasingly have the experience of *synchronicity* (discussed in the next section).

By doing this, the Artful Traveller opens their conscious awareness to the truly vast reservoir of intuitively derived knowledge that already exists at some level in their microcosmic self. In a way, it is remembering what you already know. The conditions that exist outside cause the corresponding condition inside to resonate, which is then intuitively perceived in the mind of the Artful Traveller.

The prerequisite for being more intuitive is being able to silence the incessant noise that fills the conscious minds of people living in a busy world.

To hear the still, small voice of intuition, you must create heightened awareness without the mental chatter. Breathing deeply and rhythmically helps. These last two sentences sums up the essence of meditation practice. *Heightened awareness without the mental chatter.* For a more detailed description of how to meditate in plain English, see Appendix.

Synchronicity

Synchronicity is a still-mysterious phenomenon recognized by Swiss psychologist Carl Jung. He considered it to be evidence for the existence of *archetypes* (ideal models upon which to make copies) and the *collective unconscious* (the collective mind of humanity, and by extension, the Cosmos). I prefer to call the collective unconscious the *informing principle* that underlies the universe and gives rise to the many forms that exist in it. Informing principle is close in meaning to the ancient Greek idea of Logos.

Synchronicity describes events that occur together but for which no apparent common cause can be seen. The cause is unseen; it is at the level of the collective unconscious. One can relate this to the idea of microcosm-macrocosm discussed earlier in this chapter.

Jung discussed synchronicity with Albert Einstein and Wolfgang Pauli. After these discussions, Jung came to the conclusion that there were parallels between synchronicity and relativity theory and quantum mechanics. He became very interested in exploring the idea that the phenomenal world was not a series of random events, rather that it is derived from the influence of a deeper, unseen order.

For the Artful Traveller, the benefit of knowing about synchronicity is that it draws your attention to, and leads you to a deeper awareness of the informing principle that causes the events.

Synchronicity is multi-modal in the sense that it manifests via any of the senses or on the level of thought. It could be something very ordinary, like hearing a particular word on the radio or TV, and just as you hear it, you see the same word on a sign, or see the object itself as you drive by. Or it might be a train of thought that you are having, while the same thought is expressed via some channel in your environment. It could be anything that appears connected to some other causally unrelated thing.

The experience of synchronicity is a positive sign because it indicates a movement of your ordinary awareness towards higher awareness, that part of you that is in tune with and aware of the informing principle of the macrocosm.

By recognising synchronicity and cultivating intuition, you are effectively merging your mind with the collective mind of the universe, and therefore you begin to have access to the knowledge contained in that larger mind.

This collective mind of the universe is called the informing principle in this book, but it has many names; Cosmic Mind, Universal Mind, God, Nature, Life Force. What we call it is not so important as to move beyond mere labels to the qualitative experience of it.

Communing with Nature

An excellent way to cultivate intuition is to come into a harmonious relationship with Nature. By doing so, you are aligning your inner world with the outer. In a stressful world, it is all too easy for the two worlds to become mis-aligned, out of balance. Holistic healers maintain that this misalignment is the source of disease in people.

Nature is the manifestation of the Cosmic Mind on the physical plane. There is a pervasive non-conceptual intelligence that underlies and permeates Nature and which finds expression in the billions of life-forms and intricate ecosystems that make up the biosphere of this planet.

Anyone who invests the time to know Nature is richly rewarded for their effort. To experience close communion with Nature is one of the greatest pleasures a person can have. All the more so because it is free with no strings attached.

Communing with Nature is a pathway to higher awareness (peak experiences). Nature wants you to commune with it. If you extend your mind into Nature, it will extend its mind into yours, meeting you half way, creating common ground, revealing its astonishing beauty to your Intuition. It is a truly mind expanding experience and one which requires no hallucinogenics to achieve.

Felt connectedness with all things. Peak experiences occur spontaneously when you create the right conditions in your consciousness. The foundation of this mind-set is having a sense of felt connectedness with all things. You feel that you are intimately connected with everything else in the Universe, not separate as your egoic mind would lead you to believe.

To cultivate this awareness of connectedness, remind yourself that everything in the phenomenal world is temporary. They arise from the primordial source, exist for a time, and then dissolves back into the source. There are no exceptions. You and I are an expression of this underlying source and we share the same destiny along with everything else.

A Physicist would say that in the Universe there is constant movement from energy to matter and back to energy. Imagine an animated Yin-Yang symbol with its spiral movement. Think of what a moving fractal looks like. These are representations of this constantly moving cycle. Our challenge is to not resist this movement. It is futile to try. We must make a virtue of necessity and embrace this movement wholeheartedly, surrendering to the flow.

Surrendering to the flow means letting go of the mental concepts that form the structures of your identity. Let go of them willingly before they are taken away forcibly by the movement of time. These structures were never permanent, and you need not fear losing them. They are not the real you.

Consider the Taoist metaphor that we are all swimmers in the great river of life. We can go with or against the current. The river does not mind either way. Many people swim against the current as they play their various games and become exhausted without making much progress.

The wise among us know that we are all destined to flow into the metaphoric ocean at the end of our lives, so they swim peacefully with the current, enjoying the journey and arrive at the ocean knowing that this was always their destination.

Do not worry that by swimming with the current you will arrive at the ocean too soon. The river mouth in this metaphor is not a fixed point. The ocean is reached when your life force is exhausted. By swimming with the current you achieve movement while conserving your life force.

Being Mindful. Being mindful is a state of heightened consciousness in which you experience the world around you clearly and directly, without filtering your perceptions through delusions or preconceived ideas.

Being mindful in the presence of Nature allows the subtle complexities of Nature to be revealed to your awareness and for those impressions to be received and appreciated without being distorted through judgment. It is a common mental habit for people to receive a sense perception and immediately start processing it into various categories, working on it until the conclusion bears little resemblance to external reality.

Relax and merge. Many people in the developed world are tense and stressed. Our preoccupations with the many complications of daily life create a tension that becomes the baseline of our life. But look around in Nature, most of what you see is tranquil most of the time. Nature gently flows in quietly evolving cycles from one state to its opposite. Violent explosions of energy such as storms are the exception that proves the rule that Nature is mostly tranquil.

Communing with Nature is releasing your worries and stress-producing thoughts, and, by breathing deeply you synchronise your inner world with the slower, more relaxed rhythms of Nature in the here and now. Past and future do not exist in this mind-set, only the present.

You have achieved this state of mindful presence when you are experiencing Nature in a fully conscious, non-conceptual way. It is heightened awareness without the mental chatter.

As you progress with this practice you become aware that in Nature there a vast moving river of intelligent energy all around you. This passage from Hermann Hesse's novel *Siddhartha*, illustrates the point beautifully:

However, amongst the thousands (of travellers wishing to cross the river) there have been a few, four or five, to whom the river was not an obstacle. They heard its voice and listened to it, and the river has become holy to them, as it has to me. The river has taught me to listen; you will learn from it too. The river knows everything; one can learn everything from it.

4. Being mindful

Mindfulness is a state of heightened consciousness in which a person has cultivated the mental ability to see the world around them clearly, without delusion. Seeing the world clearly requires a person to allow sense perceptions to be received but not be thought about too much.

Many people take a sense perception and immediately begin conceptualising and categorising it until a conclusion is reached after complex processing that bears little resemblance to external reality, having been filtered through the person's preconceived ideas. This process occurs more or less unconsciously in most people. Mindfulness is therefore about becoming conscious of your mind's tendency to interpret and distort meaning from your experience of the world and work to limit this tendency.

The Artful Traveller has learned to observe their mind and control how it goes. They have cultivated consciousness about consciousness. It is doubtful whether any other creature on the planet is capable of meta-awareness, since it appears to be a function of the recently evolved portions of the human brain that other animals do not have. Exercising these higher brain functions does not happen automatically in most people, it must be cultivated through right mindfulness.

Practicing mindfulness

Being fully aware in the present moment and accepting that the moment *is what it is* without wishing it was something else is the foundational mind-set for the Artful Traveller. This statement is a simple truth that takes a moment to recognise and a lifetime to master. It is also one of the basic tenets of Buddhism.

Some situations are easy to accept, others not so easy. Reclining by the pool after lunch on a warm afternoon at a five star resort is easy. Arriving at the airport to discover that an ash cloud has caused your flight to be cancelled indefinitely is a difficult reality to accept.

Accepting the reality of a undesirable situation without resistance does *not* mean taking no action, it simply means keeping a positive outlook and taking constructive action without feeling like a victim.

There is an old saying that *life may not always give you what you want, but will always give you what you need*. I used to doubt the truth of this statement until I tested it in my own life over many years. In every case that my travel plans, indeed any plans, went awry through circumstances beyond my control, I may have initially resisted it, but in every case I had valuable experiences that I would not otherwise have had. The challenge with this is learning how to transcend feeling like a victim and recognising value in people and events that we might be inclined to overlook.

So the Artful Traveller comes to see that *every moment is the best moment*. You do not wish you were somewhere else, doing something else with someone else because you think it will be somehow better. You understand that this is folly. The only time and place that you can truly be alive is right here, right now.

But I do live in the present! What are you talking about? This is often the reaction. Ask yourself honestly though, how much of your time do you *really* live in the moment? Think carefully about this; in reality most of us spend a large proportion of our waking moments thinking about past *and* future, not about what is going on in *this* moment.

Imagine you are on a city footpath. With no warning someone barges into you. Or you are driving at high speed and an accident happens not far ahead. In both cases, wherever your mind was before the event, suddenly your attention is riveted in the moment; it is a matter of survival.

In a recreational sense, imagine you are skiing fast down a snowy mountain, in the tube of a perfect wave, or any other sport that requires your complete focus in the moment and which gives you that fantastic feeling of being in the zone and nothing else matters. All of these have strong present moment awareness in common.

But when you are living your usual routine, commuting to work or sitting at your desk, how much of your attention is focussed in the Now? Probably not much, not in the same way as in the previous examples. Your attention wanders to events that happened this morning or last week; conversations, jokes, arguments and things you might have said but did not. Then your attention switches to what you might do later for fun, or what to have for dinner.

But I need to plan for the future. I also need to think of the past so I can learn from it. Yes, for practical purposes some past and future awareness is necessary. Do this if you need to, but no more than is necessary for practical purposes. Spend the rest of the time in the here and now.

The practice of mindfulness is an on-going, moment-by-moment habit. Once established, and you know that every moment you are experiencing is the best moment because it is the only *real* moment, then you have set yourself up for a peak experience in the Maslow sense, or a Satori moment in the Zen way.

Experiencing life fully, vividly, selflessly

The Artful Traveller throws themselves fully into the experience of something; concentrating on it fully, allowing it to totally absorb them.

The only way this can be done is to be (a) mindful, that is fully conscious in the present moment and (b) fully accepting of the circumstances of that moment.

This is easier said than done because most of the time we impose judgment on situations and in the process of doing so, we alienate ourselves from it. Soon we are thinking we would like to be somewhere else, doing something else, with someone else.

In terms of the Artful Traveller, mindfulness is about using an evolved part of your brain that many people do not use. It lies dormant, waiting for the command to awaken.

You can awaken this part of your brain simply by deciding (and following through on the decision) to observe the on-going activity in your own mind. Using a computer metaphor, you activate a monitoring program that watches what is going on.

This is a new dimension of thought. There is the part of you who thinks your normal thoughts, then there is the part that observes you thinking those thoughts. Previously there was only the thinker. Now there is the thinker and the observer.

Awakening the observer is an important aspect of becoming an Artful Traveller.

Mindfulness also helps you to stop thinking so much about the past and the future by removing the dimension of time from your thinking.

In the Now you observe the world of phenomena in a judgment-free way. You accept it without mental resistance, understanding that this resistance is what prevents you from

Seeing the chain of cause and effect

Mindfulness is tremendously empowering because you realise you are fully responsible for what happens in your life. It does this by raising your awareness to the point where you can see how your behaviour in the present influences what happens in your future. You can see the cause-and-effect linkages. Once you see these, you can consciously choose the behaviour that will cause a desirable future effect.

You begin to consciously engineer the shape and the content of your life. Likewise, you become aware of how you arrived in your present circumstances as a result of your previous actions.

Realising that you are ultimately responsible for what is happening around you is the real meaning of Free Will. You have the capacity to choose, but only if you are conscious enough to exercise that choice with full awareness of the implications of that choice.

The person busy ruminating on the past and worrying about the future is pre-occupied, not mindful and therefore not fully conscious. They are unlikely to see these cause and effect linkages, and will continue to behave in their habit or instinct-driven ways, indulging in self-pity and complaining that their life is such a mess and that it is everyone else's fault.

Overcoming past trauma

Mindfulness is effective remedy for putting past hurt behind you, where it belongs. If you struggle with issues that occurred in your past, whether recently or a long time ago, then mindfulness can be a great help.

Mindfulness withdraws your attention from the past and re-focuses it on the present. The painful memories will re-emerge over and over, but with persistence you can establish a new habit of being focused on the present moment. You break the cycle of having to re-live those painful events.

Post-traumatic stress and subsequent addition can be effectively remedied without drugs using mindfulness. It takes time and effort, but with commitment it has been shown to work.

One of the great challenges of this kind of recovery is to replace one's self-image as a victim with something more positive. If we have come to identify ourselves as the victim of harm, then this is who we are, despite the misery that goes it. Any identity is better than no identity.

Mindfulness creates a positive self-image by coming to see our self as a present-dwelling person who lives in and reacts to only the present. You are a person who rarely thinks about the past and who refuses to feel sorry for themselves any more. This is a tremendously liberating thing to do.

Judging versus understanding

One benefit of this judgment-free mind-set is the development of intuitive insight into people and situations. The human mind is unable to simultaneously judge *and* understand a situation. It is either one or the other. A judgmental mind-set effectively declares the matter closed, the decision made. And all of this is usually done based on the slimmest of evidence and faulty assumptions.

On the other hand, an open mind allows room for new information. It acknowledges that there is always more to people and situations than meets the eye. It effectively says *I will suspend judgment long enough to understand, then maybe I will make up my mind, or maybe I will continue to keep my mind open in case new information comes to light.*

Acceptance of what is and not minding what happens does not mean you have to put up with a bad situation and not take reasonable steps to get yourself out of that situation. It simply means coming to terms with being in that situation for the time being without resorting to anger, self-pity, accusations or other negative emotional reactions. All situations, pleasant and unpleasant, are ultimately transitory. You might as well conduct yourself with quiet dignity while the unpleasantness lasts.

The next chapter continues the Taoist perspective by discussing in detail how the principles of Taoism apply to the life of the Artful Traveller.

5. Being in harmony with the world

Knowing how to bring yourself into harmony with the world can help you to more fully experience the reality of that world. With an open, child-like mind that is ready to receive new information, your experience of the world will be fresh and exciting. One avoids having pre-conceived ideas or expectations about how the experience should be. You are almost certain to be disappointed.

This chapter outlines ways that the Artful Traveller can cultivate harmony with the world as they go about their travels. Readers familiar with Eastern philosophy may recognise some Taoist concepts here, and that is indeed the case. Taoist philosophy is a rich source of valuable information on this topic. It is essentially about learning to go with the flow.

A central idea in Taoism is avoiding extremes and always seeking the middle path on our journey through life. The objective is to negotiate the middle ground between opposites or extremes so effectively that no act is followed by a reaction. The net effect is one of neutrality. Finding the middle path means not needing to suffer the consequences of an act. In terms of the doctrine of Karma, it means knowing how to avoid bad reactions, or bad karma.

The challenge is to live this way so that we do not swing like a pendulum from one drama to the next, creating disturbances in our lives that get in the way of calm inner reflection. It is finding the Middle Path.

The Artful Traveller senses the world directly and contemplates their impressions deeply. It advises against relying on the structures and belief systems that have been created by others and put forward as orthodox truth. Such ideologies remove us from a direct experience of life and effectively cut us off from our intuition.

The Middle Path requires you to develop an awareness of the physical forces that shape our world and direct its events. Such forces operate uniformly at all levels, from the macrocosm to the microcosm. They operate in the universe as a whole and in the minds and lives of individual people. An understanding of these natural laws and the forces they direct gives a person the power to direct events in the world without resorting to force, by using attitude instead of action. Influence on others is achieved through guiding rather than ruling. The objective is always to avoid taking action that will elicit counter-reactions. In Nature, an excessive force in a particular direction tends to trigger the growth of an opposing force, and therefore the use of force cannot be the basis for establishing an enduring social condition.

The Artful Traveller comes to understand that everything in the universe is in a state of flux, and that the emotional and intellectual structures that we like to build for ourselves in order to feel secure and understand the world are likewise subject to change by external forces that are largely beyond our control. The challenge is to accept the inevitability of change and not waste our energy trying to prop up these impermanent structures, defending them against criticisms, and trying to convince others to believe in them so that they might become recognised as permanent truth.

Grasping the reality of the impermanence of all structures allows us to align ourselves with the forces of Nature that bring about incremental change in the social and physical world. We can embrace and support change whenever and wherever it wants to occur. Our alignment with the forces in Nature makes us a part of those forces. Our perceptual processes become more finely tuned because they are based on evolving reality, not on fixated thinking. We see the world as it is, not as we believe it should be.

Finding the Middle Path and keeping to it is how the Artful Traveller must arrange their life so that enough peace and tranquillity exists in their inner world. A person whose life is chaotic, lurching from one disaster to the next in a constant state of crisis is not in a state of mind conducive to experiencing Enlightenment.

Harmony with Nature

Historically, some of the longest-lived people in the East have been Taoists, or followers of the Tao. There have been numerous reliable accounts of Taoist monks living well past a century. These monks are able to do this because they live in close harmony with Nature, always seeking the Middle Path, the path of moderation, and doing nothing to extremes. The monks live their lives in such a way that their actions create no undesirable reactions.

The Tao can be a difficult concept for Westerners to understand. It is basically the name given to the abstract principle that underlies the physical world. To the Westerner, it equates to the laws of Nature or the laws of Physics. You cannot see these laws directly, but you *can* see their effect in the world. While invisible, their influence gives form and function to everything. The wise person makes the effort to study and understand what these laws are and how they work; moreover they learn to live in harmony with them.

The *Tao Te Ching* was written 2,600 years ago by the philosopher Lao Tzu. It teaches people how to achieve harmony with Nature and the evolving world. It is *not* a religious text, it is a textbook on how to understand the patterns and flows of Nature and harmonise your life with them. The version presented here is expressed in modern English, the language of the 21st Century, much easier to understand than the Chinese of 2,600 years ago.

A central idea in Taoism is to avoid extremes and always seek the middle path on our journey through life. The objective is to negotiate the middle ground between opposites or extremes so effectively that no act is followed by a reaction. The net effect is one of neutrality. Finding the middle path means not needing to suffer the consequences of an act. In terms of the doctrine of karma, it means knowing how to avoid bad reactions.

Harmony with the Tao means living so that we do not swing like a pendulum from one drama to the next, creating disturbances in our lives that get in the way of calm inner reflection. We are encouraged to sense the world around us directly and to contemplate our impressions deeply. It advises against relying on the structures and belief systems that have been created by others and put forward as fact. Such ideologies remove us from a direct experience of life and effectively cut us off from our intuition.

The Middle Path requires you to develop an awareness of the physical forces that shape our world and direct its events. Such forces operate uniformly at all levels, from the microcosm to the macrocosm. An understanding of these natural laws and the forces they direct gives a person the power to direct events in the world without needing to resort to force, by using attitude instead of action.

Influence is achieved through guiding rather than ruling. The objective is always to avoid taking action that will elicit counter-reactions. In Nature, an excessive force in a particular direction tends to trigger the growth of an opposing force. Therefore the use of force cannot be the basis for an enduring social condition.

The follower of the Tao comes to understand that everything in the universe is in a state of flux, and that the emotional and intellectual structures that we build for ourselves are likewise subject to change by external forces that are largely beyond our control. The challenge is to accept the inevitability of change and not waste our energy trying to prop up these impermanent structures.

Grasping the reality of the impermanence of all structures allows us to align ourselves with the forces of Nature that bring about incremental change in the social and physical world. Then we can embrace and support change whenever and wherever it wants to occur. Our alignment with Nature makes us a part of those forces. Our perceptions of the world become more finely tuned because they are based on evolving reality, not on orthodox thinking.

Knowing the Tao

Lao Tzu describes the behaviour and mind-set of the *enlightened person (or superior man),* by which he means the person who has attained and is living the higher standard. This advice applies directly to the attainment of long life and happiness because to achieve longevity, we must understand and emulate the Tao.

What follows is a faithful rendering into 21st Century language of the original 81 chapters of the Tao Te Ching, which was originally expressed in just 5,000 Chinese characters.

What is the Tao?

The Tao is analogous to the laws of Physics, which exist only as abstractions. The Tao cannot be seen directly, but its effects can be observed in the world of forms, hence the saying from the Tao Te Ching *the Tao that can be seen is not the real Tao.* An example of this abstraction is pi r squared, the mathematical formula for calculating the area of a circle (where pi = 22 divided by 7). This formula is an abstraction that can be applied to any circle at any scale of magnitude from an atom up to the universe itself. The formula is an example of the Tao.

Another example from Physics is Isaac Newton's second law of motion; *the mutual forces of action and reaction between two bodies are equal, opposite and collinear*. In the Tao Te Ching, this principle is discussed many times. Essentially, the enlightened person understands the operation of this law in the social sphere and ensures that any action they take is done with full awareness of the likely reactions, or, they refrain from taking action altogether.

In a general sense, the Tao can be understood as the agent by which forms evolve. It is a pervasive, underlying influence that evolves one form into its own opposite and then back again in an on-going cycle of alternating polar opposites.

Alignment with the subtle

An enlightened person works constantly to establish the Tao in their awareness, and to harmonise their mind and body with the Tao. They do not use force to achieve their ends because they know that to do so is likely to cause an equal and opposite reaction. In this way they avoid a problem of their own making. Instead, they work at the level of underlying cause and with little apparent effort are able to bring about the outcome they want. The enlightened person therefore knows that when they are in step with the Tao in worldly affairs, their endeavours can be completed efficiently and without adverse effects.

Using what is not there

Just as doors and windows cut into a wall are what make a room useful, the enlightened person knows how to use what is not there in a given situation to create a desirable effect. They create a sense of absence or need in a situation that the forces of Nature are compelled to resolve, in the same way that air rushes in to fill a vacuum.

The essence

The essence of the Tao is formless, nameless and intangible, therefore it can only be perceived by the intuitive mind, not by the analytical mind. The enlightened person works to integrate both intuitive and analytical aspects of their whole mind to arrive at a comprehensive understanding of the Tao. With an intuitive understanding of the patterns of life, they can subtly influence the outcome of events.

You do not have a life, you *are* life

The millions of life-forms on this planet -- animal and plant -- are all expressions of the same life-force. This life- force lives *through* each life-form. We are possessed by the life-force, rather being the possessor of the life-force, which is an expression of the Tao. We are all subject equally to the laws of Nature that govern Life -- we are born, gather strength, reach a peak, go into decline and then die. There are no exceptions, only variations in outer form and duration of lifecycle. The same can be said of the weather, politics, relationships and everything else in the observable world.

These laws of Nature -- the Tao -- are also expressed on a higher level in our minds and in the patterns of our social behaviour. Enlightened people gain influence by learning to live in harmony with these underlying laws of Nature. That way, they can predict future trends and take early action, placing them in the right place at the right time.

The origins of creativity

The Tao that underlies and gives shape to space and time in the world of form is the same state that preceded the Big Bang. As such it is a potent creative force. The enlightened person accesses creativity by identifying with the Absolute - the creative state that exists outside of time and space and which preceded the Big Bang. This can be done by regular meditation practice as described in an earlier chapter.

Greatness

The Tao is great because it is cyclic. It causes everything in Nature to behave cyclically. Given enough time, patterns of events repeat themselves, hence the expression 'history repeats'. The power of Taoism lies in perceiving and understanding the patterns of change and in aligning oneself with them. Enlightened people intuitively perceive the evolution of society. With sufficient patience they are able to guide themselves and others towards harmony and fulfilment. This idea is expressed by T.S. Eliot in his poem Little Gidding; *we shall never cease from exploration, and the end of all our exploring, will be to arrive where we started, and know the place for the first time.*

An evolutionary force

The Tao is an informing principle that permeates everything in the physical world, giving it structure and prescribing behavioural patterns. Over time, this informing principle interacts dynamically with the environment resulting in evolutionary changes in those life-forms as they become better adapted to their environment.

Enlightened people express the Tao and allow it to work through them. Lao Tzu believed that to emulate the behaviour of the Tao in one's own behaviour would bring a person into the closest possible alignment with reality. A life that shares, in its aims, the purpose of the universe, will also share in its greatness and significance. The enlightened person's life comes to embody the universe and charismatically demonstrates that the macrocosm (universe) is reflected in the microcosm (person).

Polarity

The Tao operates through polarity, the physical law that governs cause and effect. The law of polarity is similar to Newton's third law of motion in which every action has an equal and opposite reaction that is prescribed by the initiating cause. An initiating event in time morphs into its own opposite. A pendulum swings to one side, then to the other. In human terms this manifests in such cycles as war and peace, economic boom and bust, ignorance and enlightenment, love and hate, easy and hard.

The law of polarity changes and evolves all things by reducing extremes back to a more moderate state on its way to the opposite extreme. Extremes are by definition overcharged and must begin moving in their opposite direction. Those who follow the Tao therefore work hard to avoid extremes. They practice moderation and openness to change as a way of life.

Proactive not reactive

The enlightened person looks for the seeds of change, those underlying triggers of change that will tell them what is likely to happen in the future. Guiding them is their awareness that everything in the phenomenal world will be transformed into its own opposite in time. For example birth to death, happy to sad, strong to weak, day to night. In this way, they come to understand the movement of polarity in its countless manifestations, and so gain penetrating insight into worldly affairs. The enlightened person can proactively use this insight to position themselves favourably for when the future arrives.

For example, when we look at European history from the year 1000 to 2000, we see a pattern of aggregation. From a multitude of small states in the 11th Century has emerged a unified Europe in the 21st Century. Through cycles of war and peace, ignorance and enlightenment, plague and prosperity we see the numerous smaller states have become increasingly aggregated. Consider the unification of the German States under Bismarck and again in 1990. This movement of the Tao from war to peace to war many times has evolved Europe into a single entity. In the 21st Century this unification process is extending East to the Islamic world and South to the shores of Africa, areas not previously thought of as 'European'. Given this trend towards unification, an enlightened person might reasonably predict that the Europe Union will continue to incorporate non-EU states until it becomes necessary to change the name 'European' or at least redefine what 'Europe' means.

Another example is the rise and fall of political and commercial empires. History has many examples of empires that began modestly, rose to great power, then declined when their power spent itself.

Using the Tao is about understanding the patterns of the past, extrapolating them into the future and using this information to guide our actions in the present. In this way, we can engineer the future.

The ineffable cause

Every culture has some concept of the Ineffable (that which defies logical definition) whose purpose is to describe the underlying cause of the universe and the world as we know it. The Tao *is* that ineffable cause regardless of the name it is given.

The metaphor of a flowing river in which we all swim is often used to describe the Tao, whose movement can be seen at many levels. There is the flow of life from one day to the next, the flow of human history measured in centuries, and the flow of evolution itself, measured in millions of years. The enlightened person seeks detachment by concentrating on the underlying cause of the flow, and not on the surface phenomena.

The patterns of Nature

Enlightened people ceaselessly observe the patterns of Nature and work to bring their own behaviour into alignment with those patterns. Over time, the enlightened person's knowledge of these patterns evolves into an integrated model. This model informs their world-view with a vast network of connections that brings them into close alignment with the ways of Nature, which by definition leads to a condition of least resistance to the world.

Using the Tao to become more conscious

This section explores the action of the Tao as it manifests in human awareness. It can be used to develop one's consciousness to a level more conducive for the attainment of enlightenment and long life.

Sameness of bearing

The Tao is impartial. It does not play favourites. The human equivalent is *sameness of bearing* in which the enlightened person acts equally, with compassion, towards all people, regardless of rank or status. Sameness of bearing allows the enlightened person to achieve a degree of emotional and intellectual independence from the world, lest they be swayed to favour one person over another, one group over another. An impartial mind-set allows the enlightened person to be in tune with their intuition -- the inner voice of the Tao and the source of all creativity and enlightenment.

Being non-competitive

The behaviour of enlightened people is often compared to that of water. It is in the nature of water to seek the low places and bring benefits there. Water does not seek the high places; neither does the enlightened person seek high status for its own sake.

The conventional view of success in Western society is a competitive struggle for pre-eminence in a chosen field. A person fights their way as high as they can up the 'slippery pole', perhaps climbing over the backs of others in the process. Such competitive behaviour is a form of war-fare in which others are enemies and a person's awareness of the Tao is diminished or absent altogether. They cannot hear their inner voice, their intuition.

The enlightened person therefore cultivates a non-competitive mindset in which they look for win-win opportunities in their dealings with others. Such a mind-set expands their awareness to the point where they see no need to follow societal conventions in their quest for fulfilment.

Limiting sensual desire

The enlightened person cultivates intuition by disciplining themselves to limit their desire for sensory experiences. That desire causes attachment which causes suffering is well known as the second noble truth of Buddhism. Freeing oneself of the desire for unnecessary food, drugs, possessions and experiences brings the enlightened person into closer contact with their inner nature.

The enlightened person also limits their desire for the praise and acceptance of others. In so doing, they lessen in direct proportion the fear they might experience at the disapproval or blame of others. Praise and blame are two sides of the same coin with which our compliance with group norms is purchased.

Limiting sensual desire and expanding one's awareness to embrace the world brings your inner world into harmony with the outer. Instead of being consumed by narrow self-interest, the enlightened person's sense of identity expands to encompass the world. Such expanded awareness is the basis for enlightenment.

A true win-win situation

The enlightened person raises their consciousness by cultivating a strong desire to *know* the Tao at a deep level. The Tao reciprocates these efforts by meeting the seeker half-way. In the process, both are expanded and merge into one, producing a true win-win situation.

Perhaps this is the origin of the Biblical adage that the *Good Lord helps those who help themselves.* Philosopher Friedrich Nietzsche put it another way; *If you stare into the Abyss long enough, the Abyss stares back at you.* Abyss in this context implies immense depth, not some lurking entity.

Merge with the cycles of Nature

Everything in the universe behaves cyclically. All living creatures and inanimate things have their cycles of existence, and collectively these cycles form a vast, harmonious whole; a true miracle to behold. The enlightened person strives to know themselves as blended with this harmonious whole. They try to transcend ordinary egoic consciousness which has them separate from the world, a lone entity in a hostile wilderness.

Instincts and intuition

In the Taoist view, human instincts are fundamentally good, acting as a link to a person's intuition. When a person loses contact with their instincts, standards of right-behaviour and morality are created by society to compensate for the resulting social disarray. People are separated from their intuition when they identify themselves too much with righteous behaviour, morality and patriotism.

Consider the practice of philanthropy. Some of what passes for philanthropy in the world is primarily an attempt to buy people's good opinion. The giver is often a ruthless tycoon who has made enemies on their way to financial success. How many celebrity philanthropists would give as much if they were obliged to do so anonymously? True philanthropy does not draw attention to itself.

Contemplating the subtle

Contemplating the Tao does not appeal to the senses. Doing so will seem boring and pointless to the person who lives for sensual gratification and who expects to be entertained every minute of the day. Yet the enlightened person perseveres with this endeavour, since to do so leads to a mind-expanding glimpse and then a growing vision of the universe as a cohesive whole.

Since the laws of Physics have allowed life to evolve on this planet, it is reasonable to conclude that there is life on other planets, since the laws of Physics operate uniformly in the universe. If those laws have caused life to evolve here, then why not elsewhere? As one Cosmologist suggests, about one out of every 14,000 planets in our galaxy have conditions similar to those on planet Earth. With billions of planets in the Milky Way, there are millions of planets in this galaxy alone that could support life similar to that on Earth. And the

Milky Way is just one galaxy out of trillions in the universe. Our contemplation of the subtle leads us to conclude that there is almost certainly intelligent life out there, somewhere.

Influence without motive

The best kind of influence to exercise in worldly affairs is power without ulterior motive. Such power acts for the greater good, not personal gain. Exercising power for personal gain is perilous, since it often degenerates into the application of force, requiring elaborate strategies and manipulations to succeed.

Lao Tzu thought that morality and proprietary behaviour comes about when people are unable to see the truth in themselves, and are therefore incapable of trusting others to find truth in themselves. The problem with these forms of behaviour is that they become an entrenched block to people's ability to access the deeper truths in themselves. Then the behaviour becomes an end in itself, not a means to an end.

The enlightened person does not seek coercive power over others. Such power is ultimately self-defeating. They seek instead to become the master of subtle influence which does not appear to be power at all. This influence derives from being in close identification with the deeper reality of life.

Avoiding extremes and full maturity

When anything reaches its peak, or fullest expression, it is bound to go into decline not long afterwards. The enlightened person avoids pushing anything to an extreme state unless they deliberately want to cultivate a state of decline. This might be strategically desirable sometimes.

When a vessel is half-full it has further use and potential. When completely full it waits only to be emptied. An open-ended situation has the capacity for continued growth. A closed situation is finished.

By avoiding extremes, the enlightened person becomes increasingly centred and tranquil. In this state they are able to contribute positively to the collective awareness of the world, thus expanding their own consciousness and that of the people around them.

The flame that burns twice as bright burns half as long

The enlightened person extends their life-span through practicing moderation in all things. They limit what comes in through their senses by avoiding excessive sense stimulation. They know that their life force grows stronger if they use the moderated energy received through their senses for internal growth, so they do not talk or otherwise express too much. They practice moderation so that output does not exceed input, knowing that as life goes out, death comes in.

By nurturing their life force, the enlightened person makes themselves less vulnerable to the dangers of the world. They are protected from harm not through luck but through avoiding the cultivation of weakness. They know that the flame that burns twice as bright burns half as long.

Dwelling at the centre

Through careful observation of the patterns of Nature, the enlightened person comes to perceive the fullness of the Tao. When the Tao is perceived, a person's fears disappear as the mind expands to embrace the interconnected whole.

Lao Tzu suggests that the enlightened person should remain open to the information that comes through their senses from the outside world. They should then use their intuition to process this moderated input to develop an understanding of the patterns of life. They continually augment their experience of the world with information from their intuitive mind. They live with full awareness of the world, but habitually use intuition as their main way of understanding the world. They do not rely on theories and ideologies originating from outside to understand the world.

For example, imagine a married man goes into a bar for a drink at the end of the working day. It is a topless bar, and the sight of the barmaid's breasts causes the man to instinctively want to have sex with her. This information from his senses and his reaction to it could be intuitively understood as Nature giving the man a reason and a desire to reproduce. If the man understands this, he has no reason to feel guilty unless he acts on the desire and breaks his marriage vows. But if he references an external ideology that says such feelings are always guilt-worthy, then his guilt on this occasion will be added to the by-now crippling store of guilt that he has built up over time. The intuitive man has a clear conscience. The ideologue is burdened with guilt from having had a natural feeling. Who would you rather be? Is it not better to understand life using intuition rather than an ideology as your primary means of understanding?

Envisaging a better world

The enlightened person expands their awareness by imagining an ideally functioning world with fully conscious people living in well-founded communities. Over time, with effort, this microcosmic view of the world created in the enlightened mind can be transferred and generalised into the macrocosm.

Lao Tzu himself envisaged a world of fully conscious people who are firmly in control of their own destinies and that of the world around them. In this ideal world, all are united into a collective, compassionate entity. The Tao Te Ching is the means by which Lao Tzu is helping to bring about such a world.

Oneness with the evolving universe

Those who know, don't say; those who say, don't know is an oft-quoted passage from the Tao Te Ching. The enlightened person's understanding of the world comes from their intuitive mind and the natural structures and patterns of the universe as they are microcosmically represented in the person. This understanding is not easily translated into words, so most of the time; the enlightened person is content to simply know and feels no need to speak of it.

But if a person's understanding of the world is based on ideologies or socio-cultural artefacts of some kind, these have been formalised into words that are spoken often from one to another. This is not to imply that such an understanding is necessarily wrong. It suggests only that such an understanding runs the risk of being out of date, or incomplete, or misunderstood.

The enlightened person therefore expands their awareness by cultivating an intellectual independence that resists external influences. They realise their oneness with the evolving universe through unwavering simplicity and inner truth.

The disease

There is a common stereotype in the world of the highly educated specialist who is not interested in what others have to say because they believe they know everything worth knowing already.

The enlightened person knows that regardless of how much knowledge they have, there is still much they do not know, and will probably never know, so vast is the overall knowledge accumulated by humanity over time. So they maintain humility about their erudition and remain open to new information from the changing world regardless of the status of the person imparting that information.

In the Taoist view, it is considered most unfortunate to be unaware of one's ignorance, whether in interpersonal matters, worldly affairs or within the self. So the enlightened person cultivates the attitude of the beginner who knows little and is open to new ideas from a constantly evolving universe that they are yet to experience.

By maintaining this beginner's attitude, the enlightened person avoids the inevitable decline that comes from being too full to grow any further.

Using the Tao to cultivate oneself

The enlightened person lowers their expectations to the point where they are rarely if ever disappointed and often delighted. They understand that much of the unhappiness in the world is the result of people's expectations not being met. Expectations are a burden that the enlightened person discards like a heavy sack that they carry on their back.

The enlightened person also frees themselves from their pre-conceived ideas and any ideologies that might limit their growth. They understand that belief systems have a use by date, that the zeitgeist that produced them is evolving. What was once appropriate and functional becomes less so over time. They simply keep an open mind and react to the reality of the present moment without filtering their perception through the lens of pre-conceived ideas.

The pendulum of polarity

The enlightened person understands that the world of form is characterised by polar opposites that oscillate back and forth between the two ends of the same continuum. It is not possible to have one without the other. When beauty is present, ugliness is not far away. Youth gives way to maturity. Happiness turns into sadness. Wealth becomes poverty. Arrogance becomes humility. The Sufi proverb *This too shall pass* expresses this essential truth with forceful simplicity.

The enlightened person also knows that matter becomes energy which then becomes matter again in an eternal cycle of creation and destruction. All of the physical forms in the world, in the universe, will cease to exist in a physical sense one day and return to energy only to revert to matter again at a later time.

Descending from the peak

When the enlightened person achieves success, they do not *rest on their laurels* and wait for the inevitable decline. Instead they move quickly on to the next challenge and continue their growth even though this involves descending from the peak that was so laboriously attained, down into the valley that lies before the next peak. They avoid accumulating social ties and/or material possessions, all of which can reduce their ability to move on to the next challenge.

Moderating the dynamic tension between polar opposites

Human nature is comprised of a complex set of oscillating polar opposites. These can push and pull a person here and there, contributing to the drama and sometimes chaos in their lives. The enlightened person works hard to moderate the extremes of these oscillations, endeavouring to stabilise them on or near the Middle Path, thus creating a calm inner space in which contemplation can occur. This is an important skill on the spiritual path.

Subtle influence

The enlightened person develops their ability to perceive an unfolding situation at a deep level. They take no action unless they have first come to this understanding. The only way they can do this is to harmonise their inner self with the outer situation, aligning their inner reality with the outer.

Having perceived the unfolding pattern, the enlightened person moves forwards with modesty and a stability that causes no counter reactions. The less obvious their actions are, the more effective they become. To the world they appear to be reserved. They channel their influence to bring clarity and cooperation into the world.

For example, if a dictator seizes power in a *coup d'etat*, the natural tendency is for the people resist and the dictator must spent considerable energy dealing with this reaction to his initial action. If, on the other hand, he were to work quietly, from within the existing government to bring about evolutionary change, it would barely be recognised by the people and the change of government would seem like a natural progression.

Independent perspective

Lao Tzu suggests that having an independent perspective is vital for spiritual growth. The enlightened person keeps their own counsel, removing themselves from situations where group-think exerts its influence. With independence of thought they shed their misgivings and can explore the universe with no preconceived ideas. Independence of thought means divesting oneself of ideological thinking and orthodox sets of belief. It takes courage to do this. Humans tend to be social creatures with a powerful instinct for group-thinking, a vestige of our evolutionary past where there was safety in numbers and consensus promoted survival. The person who moves out of the orthodoxy is likely to be punished by the group for their non-conformist thinking. Often this will be enough to bring the person back into the fold where it is comfortable and secure. But at some level they know they have traded their freedom for this security.

Unhindered by group-think and with a clear perception of the world as it is, the enlightened person makes a significant contribution to the collective awareness of human-kind. They see the likely future by extrapolating upon the patterns of the past. As Einstein observed *we cannot solve problems by using the same kind of thinking we used when we created them.*

Observing the patterns of Nature

Lao Tzu noticed that the patterns of Nature are evident in socio-cultural behaviour. For example the pattern of cause and effect is clearly evident everywhere in Nature *and* in the human social environment. The enlightened person works hard to transcend cause and effect by practicing moderation. For example, an obvious attempt to gain power is avoided, since to do so is likely to produce a neutralising effect in the social environment. The enlightened person exerts influence by channelling the inner power that comes from having a universal awareness. They achieve their objectives by avoiding showy outer appearances.

Through this practice, enlightened people develop what might be called intellectual gravity, the exercise of which can determine the direction of society. The stronger the gravity, the greater the influence will be.

The conventional wisdom of society encourages people to display themselves. Yet such a display is by definition excessive. In Nature excess is naturally reduced. The enlightened person realises it is ill-advised to seek prominence. It is better to exert subtle influence behind the scenes. In this way, they achieve stability and longevity. By working behind the scenes, the laws of Nature do not act to reduce their position.

For example, consider the musician Kurt Cobain. He became famous, but found the fame intolerable. He had become that which he despised. To Kurt, the only way to resolve his dilemma was to commit suicide, which he did in 1994. Celebrity status did not bring happiness or enlightenment to Kurt, just intolerable sadness that could only be resolved through oblivion.

Steady, incremental improvement

As a general rule, slow change is preferable to radical change. The former can be sustained for long periods; the latter quickly leads to exhaustion. The enlightened person therefore acts sustainably and avoids confrontation or aggressive movement towards their objectives. They know that in Nature, the sudden intense storm is the exception to the rule, that most of the time Nature operates in a steady, harmonious way that brings about gradual transformation, almost imperceptibly. The enlightened person therefore practices steady, incremental improvement over time, and achieves their objectives harmoniously.

Cultivating the steady force of positive attitude and expressing it modestly gives the enlightened person a degree of personal power. They know that what they think and believe is what they will become, in time.

Mastery of self

Insight into the underlying causal patterns beneath socio-cultural phenomena can be had through self-knowledge and self-discipline. The enlightened person works hard to know their inner mind. In time, they come to see the connection with the evolving mind of the universe. With self-mastery, the enlightened person can make a lasting contribution to society.

Self-mastery and the insight that follows give the enlightened person the ability to change the world through small, effortless actions at the beginning of events before the situation has become more settled. A prime example is a wise and benevolent parent giving their impressionable child much information about the world and how it works at a time when the child is still open to such messages. This effort by the parent for 20 or more years sets the child up for the rest of their life, perhaps another 70 years.

Needing less

Material possessions *can* be an impediment to spiritual growth. The problem is not in the having of possessions as such. The problem arises when a person *identifies* with their possessions, creating a sense of identity like a King identifying with his palaces and kingdom, a CEO with his organisation. Their intellectual growth is slowed because the forms which occupy their thinking are relatively unchanging. They are required to spend considerable effort in maintaining those forms, and preventing the theft of them. Over time, materialistic people come to regard the world as being fixed into specific forms. In reality though, Nature is fluid and evolving. The enlightened person therefore does not create an identity for themselves from their possessions. They know that by doing so, they reduce their ability to move freely with the spirit of the times.

Animals and plants display the power of needing less. They have little except their lives and the environment that sustains them. They are in harmony with the Tao and need nothing more for their survival.

Keeping an open mind

A mind that remains open to new information on a moment by moment basis is a pre-requisite for spiritual growth. A person seeking enlightenment works daily to overcome the all-too-human tendency to settle into an established belief system that they have been investing in for years or decades. The more invested a person feels themselves to be, the more closed-minded they become to information that does not agree with their beliefs, or which threatens those beliefs in some way.

Such a belief system may have been correct in the past, but in an evolving social environment those ideas probably need updating. An open mind stays in harmony with the collective mind of society and the universe. It is from this position of openness and harmony with the universe that the enlightened person acts upon the world in a way that does not create negative reactions.

Lao Tzu speaks of a powerful transformative practice. By loving people who do not love themselves, the enlightened person emulates the Tao and neutralises the negative attitudes of others. Lao Tzu considered that the ability to neutralise extremes in their various forms is the way to transform the world into a more peaceful place.

The mind of humanity, the group mind, is an intermediate step between our individual mind and the universal mind. The group mind is a stepping stone that the enlightened person can use to perceive the larger universal mind. It allows them to go beyond and see themselves in relation to the universe. They merge their individual mind with the group mind by first *opening* their mind, and allowing their sense of identity, their ego, to be diminished. The difficulty is that the ego protects itself with a host of effective defence mechanisms.

Dwelling in the Tao

Since only the ruling elite could read, the Tao Te Ching was written for an exclusive readership; those whose destiny was to lead or otherwise influence worldly affairs. The book teaches how to cultivate intuition. With an intuitive understanding, the reader could perceive the evolution of society and be in a position to positively influence that evolution. It should be remembered that China at the time of writing was a war-torn land, badly in need of a moderating influence.

Remaining flexible and adaptable

The enlightened person recognises from his or her observations of Nature that flexibility and adaptability is necessary for long-term survival. The universe is evolving, and everything in it is changing. Therefore people who hold fixed, orthodox beliefs are not likely to react appropriately to new challenges.

Imagine a sapling tree growing on a wind-swept hill. Nearby is the sapling's mature parent. When the winter gales blow, the young tree bends. After the storm, it resumes its upright position. But the old tree has become inflexible, unable to bend. One day, it simply snaps and falls over.

On a human level, young people display adaptability to their world that allows them to adjust. But as they grow older, some of them become overly attached to their youth and resist the changes happening around them. They are heard complaining about the state of the world, and how they would like to go back to the 'good old days'. These are the same good old days when it was considered good practice to physically punish women and children.

As they age, they resemble the inflexible old tree that will inevitably collapse in the face of some adversity. But it need not happen. An enlightened elderly person accepts the need to change with the times. They are prepared to let go of out-moded beliefs, and are willing to expend the effort to learn new skills. They do not criticise the younger generation for simply believing differently than they do. In short, they make the effort to stay young when it is easier to grow old.

The great leveller of extremes

The enlightened person has observed Nature's way of levelling extremes. An example on a grand scale is the magnificent Himalayan Mountains. Through tectonic collision of the Earth's crust the Himalayas were raised. The mountains reach great heights, but through the further movement of the Tao over millions of years, the mountains are being worn away by the weather. Rushing melt-water erodes the mountainsides every year. Billions of tonnes of alluvium then wash down the Ganges and Brahmaputra rivers, settling in the spreading delta and out into the Bay of Bengal where it becomes sea-bed. What was high is now low.

An animal that breeds too prolifically and becomes a plague is naturally reduced to smaller numbers in time. In human affairs, a tyrant eventually gets their come-uppance. At the molecular level, atoms form bonds with each other that allow for the mutual reduction of excess electrical charge. Everywhere in Nature we see this moderating influence of the Tao.

The enlightened person uses this principle to safe-guard their own position while they go about their work of improving society. In order for energy to flow in their direction, they maintain a modestly reduced position by being humble in their dealings with others and avoiding shows of ostentation.

For example, if someone with sufficient means were to quietly donate $1,000 a month to an international welfare agency, they might bring benefit to perhaps 1,000 people in the developing world in the form of clean drinking water, improved agriculture, schools, basic hospital care etc. This gift would be greatly appreciated by the mother who has already lost a baby to dysentery and cannot bear to lose another but fears she will. The same $1,000 might also be used to buy a flashy consumer item for the purpose of raising the owner's social status. The enlightened person sees the relative merit in these two scenarios.

Being magnanimous

When the enlightened person has power over others, they know to act with generosity and compassion. Not gloating over their advantage avoids the possibility of lingering resentment that may adversely affect their future dealings. Through generosity, they create a mind-set of appreciation and agreement in people, which is all the better for collaborative endeavours.

It is said that the best kind of leader is barely known, the next best is known and loved, while the worst kind is leader is known and despised. People have a natural enmity towards unjust authority figures. To avoid the possibility of being perceived as unjust, the enlightened leader keeps a low profile such that they their existence or at least their influence are barely perceived.

Living for the maximum benefit of others

Simple, plain truth that is not embellished with sophistry and rhetoric is unlikely to become distorted. The enlightened person therefore maintains an attitude of simplicity. They conduct their affairs and express themselves with simplicity. This attitude cultivates a mind-set that sees clearly the truth in a given situation. They allow their actions to speak for themselves, knowing that people instinctively know that a person's actions speak louder than their words.

Simplicity extends to not hoarding static accumulations of possessions or money for the love of having them, rather than using them for worthwhile purposes. The enlightened person avoids hoarding and keeps the flow of energy moving through their life. By not accumulating an extreme amount, they do not invite the levelling influence of the Tao.

The enlightened person lives to do the maximum good in the most unobtrusive way. Their reward is not recognition from society but the deep satisfaction of knowing that one is emulating the Tao and is thereby in harmony with it.

Using the Tao to lead others

Leadership is seeing a compelling future and communicating your vision of that future in a way that creates enthusiasm. The Taoist perspective is useful with this since it cultivates a strong awareness of the patterns of Nature and how these influence human societies. With this awareness you can extrapolate these patterns into the future and see what is possible. But the future is not set in stone. Its direction is influenced by the visionaries and their ability to make their vision a reality.

Consider for example the visions of the future created by the early science fiction writers Jules Verne and H.G. Wells. Generations of engineers have been inspired by the works of Verne and Wells, producing all manner of technologies from submarines called *Nautilus* that could travel 20,000 leagues under the sea without surfacing, journeys to the moon and back, and the exploration of Mars. Later sci-fi writers like Philip K. Dick and William Gibson have also had a profound effect on the direction of technology development. Regardless of form and content, all of these writers imagined a compelling future and communicated it to the world with impact.

Regardless of whether you are a manager of other people, or someone who has less formal relationships with those around them, the principles discussed in this section describe the Taoist way of influencing people. Lao Tzu wrote the Tao Te Ching for those who might help create a better world. Even if you are a hermit who has little or no contact with the world of people, these ideas will help you to become an effective leader of yourself, if not others.

The steady force of attitude

Leading by example is the most desirable form of leadership. The enlightened leader understands that it is the steady force of their attitudes, as perceived by those around them, that exerts the greatest influence, more so than their actions or their words. Through example, people come to know what a leader respects and values. These values become the motivating force behind people's actions. The enlightened leader therefore models high regard for honesty, flexibility and spontaneity.

The enlightened leader avoids championing high-achievers. They know that by creating one winner, they simultaneously create multiple losers who then feel under-valued. High achievers should be *quietly* congratulated and rewarded. Singling high-achievers out for public praise creates what Stephen Covey calls a scarcity mentality. The praise of the leader is a scarce commodity that is reserved for the favoured few.

The enlightened leader brings peace and stability to the group through the steady force of their positive attitudes. They do not micro-manage, allowing people to get on with their activities without interference.

Subtle influence

According to Lao Tzu, the best kind of leader is one whose existence is barely known by those they lead. The next best are loved, the next are respected and the next are ridiculed.

The enlightened leader avoids coercion, instead they use subtle influence (like goal-setting, trust and carefully worded directives) so that the people are barely aware of their influence. The worst thing a leader can do is adopt and overbearing approach in which people perceive that they are being interfered with at some level and their need for autonomy is disregarded. This is sure to generate negative reaction.

Subtle influence allows a person to develop autonomy from which they derive the satisfaction of one who manages their own affairs.

Maintaining simplicity

Simple, intuitively-derived ways of behaving that are in tune with the Tao are preferable to socially-defined behaviour protocols. It is all too easy with the latter to make mistakes and give unintentional offence. Correct behaviour protocols create in-groups and out-groups, those who know how to behave correctly, and the uncouth oafs who do not. It plays into the egoic tendency to categorise the world as *us and them, friend and enemy*. Simple, intuitively based leadership is likely to be more inclusive and compassionate, seeking commonality between people rather than points of difference.

Modes of social behaviour that are considered praiseworthy, such as self-seeking philanthropy, should be avoided. Self-seeking behaviour of any kind is primarily done for social recognition that then feeds back to improved self-esteem. It is an indication that Intuition is not being used and the person needs an external source to tell them what is right and good. The enlightened leader, in tune with their intuition, practices anonymous philanthropy and enhances their self-esteem directly.

The enlightened leader therefore acts with humility and remains in close contact with their instincts. They keep their thoughts and actions simple and spontaneous. With this mind-set, they are more agile and appropriate in their responses to emerging situations. Simplicity endows power through clarity of meaning. People intuitively perceive the enlightened leader's alignment with the Tao.

The enlightened leader therefore throws off the constraints of orthodoxy and tradition, using these only in a secondary sense, if at all. Orthodoxy can be a strait-jacket for the imagination. It constrains creativity and limits spontaneity. A tradition-bound leader will tend to base their decisions on precedent *what did my predecessors do in this situation* or *in 1793, our illustrious leader did this in response to a similar situation?*. These prefabricated responses lack insight and run a high risk of not being appropriate for the situation at hand.

Gravitas

Gravitas, or force of personality can exercise strong influence on people, so it is wise to know how to cultivate it. Gravitas is manifested in the enlightened leader as they become more closely aligned with the Tao. Such alignment naturally deepens and endows perceived substance to their personality.

It has been observed that the worth of a nation, or organisation or individual can be known by how they treat the weakest member of their group. Observe how a person treats those over whom they have power. Do they treat them with consideration and respect, or are they harsh because they can be? The enlightened leader knows that treating everyone with simple dignity endows their actions with subtle but powerful influence; the underlying quality of gravitas. Author John Steinbeck demonstrated true leadership with his Nobel Prize winning novel *The Grapes of Wrath* (1939). In contrast, French Queen Marie-Antoinette from her privileged position showed contemptuous disregard for the welfare of the people with her *let them eat cake* comment. Though probably a journalistic cliché it sums up the attitude of the French aristocracy that so enraged the people and led to the French Revolution in 1789.

Enlightened leaders do not use their position to grant themselves special rewards not available to everyone, for example executive bonuses that are many times the annual salary of ordinary employees. The simple dignity of the servant leader is most conducive to achieving their objectives.

Coordinating collective effort

Enlightened leadership is seen where the talents and abilities of diverse people are coordinated into a unified effort. It is creating an environment in which people can network and exchange ideas in pursuit of common objectives. The leader is like a lake that collects water. They provide the environment in which people can work together and exchange ideas in pursuit of common objectives. Their influence is so pervasive and subtle that people stop noticing.

Intuitive leaders therefore have the ability to unite people with diverse backgrounds into a single enterprise, thus creating a direct link between people whose only previous connection was so tenuous as to be almost invisible. The enlightened leader perceives these subtle connections and builds networks. In this way, they behave like the Tao.

Guide rather than rule

People dislike being forced to do anything. They want freedom to choose, or at least the appearance of freedom. So even when an enlightened leader has the authority to order people about, they avoid doing so. It is better to guide people by giving them a reason to want to do it.

As Dwight Eisenhower remarked, leadership *is the art of getting people to do what you want them to do because they want to do it.* The enlightened leader does this by presenting the case in such a way that the course of action is clearly in the person's best interest.

Cultivating one-ness

The enlightened leader recognises the inter-connectedness of all things in the universe and cultivates a sense of solidarity and oneness with people. This oneness is a state of felt awareness and harmony between the one and the many. The enlightened leader works daily to cultivate this sense of felt connectedness with everything. It gives insight into the rhythms and patterns of the Universe and informs the enlightened leader's every action.

Unity of effort

Unity of effort is achieved when the enlightened leader creates enthusiasm for their vision of the future. They put the right person in the job, provide the resources they need, the authority to make decisions, then stand back and let them do the work without unnecessary restrictions.

Lao Tzu believed that people are basically good at heart, only becoming aggressive and unruly in reaction to unreasonable force or perceived injustice. The enlightened leader therefore fosters a collaborative environment based on fairness and behaves with simplicity and modesty. They avoid creating unnecessary internal competition which works against collaboration by encouraging people to pursue strategies to gain advantage at the expense of others.

Replace rigid rules with spontaneity

Some organisations operate with rigidly defined rules that everyone must conform to if they are not to be sanctioned. This approach offends human nature with its unreasonable force. The consequence is that the people grow resentful and look for ways to subvert the rules, and they will usually succeed at this. When management perceives the trend, they react in the only way they know how; by exerting more pressure. The people react even more strongly, and a negative cycle of behaviour is created.

Rigidly defined rules are a form of extremism that produces sharply polarised attitudes. These attitudes are likely to be counter-productive by reducing the desire to collaborate freely. The enlightened leader knows how polarity operates in Nature, and so they avoid such extremes. They achieve their objectives without confrontation, projecting a straight-forward, down-to-earth honesty that inspires trust and confidence in people, and which provides a model for the people to emulate.

Like cooking a small fish

Leading a large organisation is like cooking a small fish. This enigmatic statement conveys the need for an enlightened leader to maintain a light, delicate touch in their leadership in the same way as it is necessary to avoid too much stirring when cooking a small fish, lest the fish fall apart in the pan. When an organisation is experiencing challenges, too much action from the leader will unbalance the situation, making it worse.

The enlightened leader knows that if there is no simple solution to a problem, it is best to simply let it be and allow the forces of Nature to evolve a solution. In this culture of simplicity and non-interference, people engaging in subterfuge become apparent, and their strategies are rendered ineffective.

Uniting the group into a team

The enlightened leader makes it their business to help everyone in the organisation towards fulfilment and higher attainment, not just those that seem somehow worthy of preferment. Lesser performers are also regarded as valuable members of the group who can be helped forward with education and other opportunities. This transforms a group into a team who are united behind the leader, and in whom the desire to collaborate is strong.

Avoid Machiavellian strategies

The enlightened leader refrains from clever strategies and political manoeuvrings. They know that this sends a message to do likewise, leading to an escalating cycle of such behaviour in the organisation. The enlightened leader therefore acts with simplicity and directness and so encourages the people to do likewise.

Humility

The enlightened leader understands that to rise above people in a leadership sense, they must remain below them by acting and speaking with sincere humility. This is perceived as complete identification with the people, engendering trust because the people instinctively know that if the leader is below them, the interests of the leader will be the same as theirs. If the leader does not act superior, the people see themselves in the leader and this engenders respect, if not love.

Compassion

The best kind of leader is compassionate, modest and does not thrust themselves into prominence. Compassion in a person has a deeply transformative effect on the mind and those they come in contact with. It endows the ability to have a lasting effect on the world. The enlightened leader therefore manifests compassion in all their dealings.

Using the Tao to influence group dynamics

The factors discussed here contribute to the harmonious achievement of goals at all levels, from the family, community, to organisation, state, nation all the way up to the global the community of humanity.

Avoid self-aggrandisement

Enlightened people avoid being too visible or boastful of their achievements because there is a levelling mechanism in group psychology that naturally seeks to balance aggrandisement. Such behaviour creates excess. It creates instability in the social dynamic. Excess indicates that something has reached its peak and must by necessity go into decline. The enlightened person discretely removes themselves from the situation before the limelight shines upon them. For example, even the most popular political leader is harshly criticised by some sections of the public, regardless of how diligently they work to stay in favour.

Hypocrisy is particularly poisonous. The enlightened person carefully avoids not only being a hypocrite, but the appearance of being one. They know it is tempting to agree with people in private discussions, expressing a different opinion with each person, as a way of earning their support. But the enlightened person knows that they must maintain the integrity of their position, and not vary it between people. This sameness of bearing generates trust. Even though this may not please everyone, it does earn the enlightened person a reputation for integrity and impartiality. Often, the person of integrity pleases no-one, and is criticised for it because they refuse to take sides in a dispute. It is the only viable way to behave however, since any favours earned through double-dealing are short-lived. The friend of today becomes an enemy tomorrow. The person of integrity earns the respect of all, if not their friendship.

Avoid cunning and manipulation

Clever schemes and coercive force will often produce the opposite of what was planned, earning the person a reputation for cunning and duplicity. The enlightened person knows it is better to act with simple honesty in pursuit of one's goals, thus generating trust.

Simplicity is achieved through spontaneous, intuitive action based on an understanding of human nature and the situation at hand. This is the opposite of the Machiavellian ploy that may succeed in the short-term, but not in the mid to long-term.

Avoid aggression

Aggression in all of its forms is avoided by the enlightened person, since aggression creates excess, and excess always produces a neutralising reaction. Where affirmative action is called for, the enlightened person behaves assertively, not crossing the line between aggression and assertion. Assertion is restrained action.

Aggression in individuals and groups consumes much energy and resources, leading to resource depletion and weakening. Restrained action uses that energy constructively in the pursuit of its goals. The enlightened person knows that success does not have to come at the expense of another. The *win-win* scenario in which everyone benefits is in keeping with the Tao.

Use force only when absolutely necessary

When circumstances demand it, the use of force can be unavoidable. The enlightened person expresses regret at having to use force. They make it clear that it gives them no pleasure. As in Nature, the incidence of overwhelming force is rare (for example a tornado or earthquake). Most of the time, change is brought about through harmonious transformation.

Cultivating restraint and humility

Powerful organisations have much, but they also have much to lose. Their wealth and influence are the envy of others who want some of it for themselves. Such organisations can avoid this by cultivating modesty. They make themselves vulnerable to decline through complacency, excess, and sense of entitlement. Hubris leads them to believe they are unassailable. Any advantages the organisation possesses are kept concealed, out of sight from the external world where they will excite no envy or alarm.

Knowing how much is enough

Greed is a serious character flaw. It leads a person to not only desire more possessions, but to seek an identity for themselves in those possessions rather than focus on internal growth. When organisations are run without acquisitiveness as its central concern the internal qualities of the organisation are encouraged to grow in positive, self-improving ways. Its dealings with the world will take on a benevolent aspect which is likely to produce greater prosperity for all and limit the potential for harm.

Avoiding escalation

In any evolving social environment there will be conflict between opposing ideas. The enlightened person knows that the ideas that eventually prevail are those whose proponents have managed to avoid strong counter-reactions to the idea. They do this by avoiding aggression. Force is met with force, and strategy with strategy. Lao Tzu thought that the side that was wise enough to feel sorrow and regret at the use of force would be the side that triumphs.

Accepting blame

The enlightened person in organisations takes on the qualities of water. Soft and receptive with no edge and no form, water absorbs and transforms hard structures. By taking responsibility, including accepting the blame for situations, the enlightened person establishes their position at the centre of the organisation. They extend their influence outwards in a positive way. Blame in this context refers to that which happens inside and outside the organisation. They are able to foresee and avoid similar problems in the future.

Promoting independence

Lao Tzu considered the ideal social grouping (at every level from family to nation) to be one in which every member can reach their potential in whichever direction that takes them. They have access to health care, education and recreation; nothing short of the pursuit of happiness. Every person values their life, so they will value life-enhancing activities that they instinctively know is the way to find themselves, develop a strong sense of purpose and ultimately reach their full potential. When a person feels strong and independent they are likely to work hard, maintain good relationships and remain loyal to the organisation.

Using the Tao to refrain from action

Strategic non-action can be a powerful method of achieving lasting influence in worldly affairs. In cultures where action is favoured over inaction, direct action is considered a virtue while inaction is considered little more than laziness or cowardice. This section suggests that there is a time for both action and inaction and describes the ways in which inaction can be used to advantage.

Selflessness

Periods of action are followed by a periods of inaction. To create a situation in which action is required, the enlightened person begins with inaction to prepare the way. The transition from inaction to action then seems natural, effortless. Such a beginning to action is unlikely to attract opposition. By placing themselves last and outside, the enlightened person creates a situation where natural social forces compel them forward towards the centre, doing so with naturalness and ease. Placing themselves selflessly will align their goals more closely with the evolving social environment.

Harmony

There is an inner pattern to everything in Nature. Cells-replicate, crystals grow, societies evolve all according to a precise template that resides, unseen, within the entity. Therefore the enlightened person is careful not to interfere with natural processes, knowing that to do so would be dangerous and ultimately futile. In social systems, the enlightened person maintains a position that is in harmony with the evolutionary forces that gradually evolve that society. Their influence is subtly exerted through the force of their focussed inner awareness. Thus they often refrain from taking action when to do so would adversely impact the natural evolutionary flow.

Avoid becoming too specialised

Lao Tzu considered that increasing specialisation is ultimately self-limiting because highly specialised systems impose constraints upon participants which effectively reduces them to machines forced to follow strict procedures. In such an environment, a person stops growing, stops being creative. In Nature, species that become too specialised are prone to extinction. So too with overly specialised organisations. Better to move towards universality, away from differentiation. By looking for what is universally true, one achieves simplicity. The greater the truth, the more simply it can be expressed.

Subtle influence

Lao Tzu observed that many of the troubles of the world are reactions to earlier provocations. People or groups seek revenge, and in doing so, set up a situation in which the trouble is perpetuated. What you resist persists. By refraining from action, the trouble dissipates over time. The enlightened person therefore uses subtle influence to resolve problems by choosing a course of non-action or minimal action designed to produce no further reactions.

Strategic non-action

A deep understanding of situations is gained from one's intuition in a context of non-interference. The knowledge that derives from action is situation-specific, a deeper understanding is obscured by the interplay of action and reaction. Non-action or non-interference is therefore a strategic approach to harmonising one's inner awareness with the larger forces at work in the external world. This allows the enlightened person to instinctively know where best to position themselves to achieve their goals.

Truth in non-action

The enlightened person rids themselves of fixed ideas from the past, and centres their thinking in the Now, giving them a moment-by-moment awareness of how their social environment is evolving. This awareness reveals the possibilities that the evolving environment offers. Fixed ideas obscure such impressions. Ideally, one gains pure information from observing an environment that is not reacting to the observer in any way. If the observer is also an actor, then some of what is observed is due to the observer's own actions, leading to observational bias.

Being non-confrontational

Being infant-like is often used to describe the essence of the Tao. An infant and young child lives moment-by-moment in touch with their original nature before the layers of societal conditioning accumulate later in childhood. Because young children are clear embodiments of the Tao, the world is not inclined to harm them, nor do they struggle for wealth and power and so place themselves in harm's way. The enlightened person likewise adopts a spontaneous, natural, non-confrontational attitude towards life in order to protect themselves from harm in the world. When someone pushes them, they yield. Their opponent is thus thrown off balance and appears to the rest of the world as aggressive, which may then result in a neutralising reaction. The enlightened person concentrates on maintaining balanced energy. They know that unbalanced energy is inherently unstable and leads to its own demise.

Like a river finding its way through a valley of boulders

When the enlightened person finds themselves in the position of needing to influence an on-going event they apply their efforts to the weakest area. When the weakness absorbs the effort, the weakness moves to another location, and the enlightened person follows. In this way they avoid confrontation with an apparently insurmountable problem and so avoid the counter-reactions that derive from the confrontation. They act like a river finding its way through a valley of stones. When the water encounters a stone, it flows smoothly around it and continues on. Eventually the water wears down the stone with little apparent effort. So it is that with non-confrontational actions, the enlightened person influences an on-going event. Their restrained action causes no adverse counter-reaction and they achieve their goals with apparent ease.

Recognising the beginning

The best time to influence events is at the beginning, before they acquire momentum. The enlightened person hones their skill at recognising when a situation is at its least entrenched state, and positions themselves to guide the event through to a successful conclusion. This skill is developed by limiting their desires and avoiding dogmatic or process-driven ways of accomplishing goals.

Give me freedom or give me death

Lao Tzu believed that human nature is essentially good. To remain good-hearted though, people need to perceive themselves as being free to live their lives how they see fit, to think the way they want to think, and not to have these freedoms eroded by authority figures and governments seeking to limit their freedoms and control them. When authority becomes oppressive, people lose the fear of death and rise up to end the oppression even if they lose their lives in the process. This is how precious freedom is in the hearts of people. For example, the French, Russian and American Revolutions all derived from people finding their rulers intolerable.

The doomed leader

An insecure leader believes their personal interests are identical to the interests of the organisation. They *are* the organisation. It causes them to curtail people's freedom. They are worried that given enough freedom, the people will oust them (a not unreasonable belief).

As the regime becomes more oppressive, the people suffer. Perhaps they have to work long hours in poor conditions. Maybe people do not get enough to eat, or disease goes untreated. All the while contempt for the leader grows. There can be only one outcome – the leader's eventual demise. The enlightened leader refrains from limiting people's freedom. Instead they provide the people with the means to grow and fulfil their potential, giving them the space in which to express that potential.

6. Communing with Nature

The Artful Traveller does not spend all of their time in the built environment; the natural environment sometimes beckons. This chapter gets into some metaphysical ideas about transcendence, so if you want to keep your experience of this book down-to-earth, you could skip to the next chapter now.

Nature is the manifestation of the Divine on the physical plane. There is a pervasive non-conceptual intelligence that permeates Nature and which finds expression in the billions of life-forms and intricate ecosystems that make up the biosphere of this planet.

Anyone who invests the time to know Nature is bountifully rewarded for their effort with a deep intuitive understanding of the intricate webs of connectedness and a strong sense of oneness with it all. To experience close communion with Nature is one of the greatest pleasures a person can have. All the more so because it is free, and with no strings attached.

Nature *wants* you to commune with it. If you extend your mind into Nature, it will extend its mind into yours, meeting and merging with you, creating common ground, revealing its astonishing beauty to your intuition.

Here is how the Artful Traveller can deepen their experience of the natural environment by merging their mind with the larger mind of Nature, becoming one with it.

Felt-connectedness with all things

Enlightenment occurs spontaneously when you create the right conditions in your life. The foundation of this mind-set is having a sense of felt connectedness with all things. You feel that you are intimately connected with everything else in the Universe, not separate as your egoic mind would lead you to believe. Enlightenment occurs when your consciousness transcends the world of separate forms, and experiences the connected reality that lies appearances.

To cultivate this awareness of connectedness, remind yourself that all entities in the Universe are temporary. They arise from the primordial source, exist for a time, and then dissolve back into the source. There are no exceptions. You and I are an expression of this underlying source and we share the same destiny as everything else.

A Physicist would say that in the Universe there is constant movement from energy to matter and back to energy. Imagine an animated Yin-Yang symbol with its spiral movement. Think of what a moving fractal looks like. These are representations of this constantly moving cycle. Our challenge is to not resist this movement. It is futile to try. We must make a virtue of necessity and embrace this movement wholeheartedly, surrendering to the flow.

Surrendering to the flow means letting go of the mental concepts that underpin your sense of identity. Let go of them willingly instead of clinging to them until they are taken away forcibly by the movement of time. These structures were never permanent, and you need not fear losing them. They are not the *real* you.

Consider the Taoist metaphor of being swimmers in the great river of life. We can go with or against the current. The river does not mind either way. Many people swim against the current as they enact their various dramas and become exhausted without making much progress, their lifeless bodies eventually floating out to sea.

The wise among us know that we are all destined to flow into the ocean at the end of our lives, so they swim peacefully with the current, enjoying the journey and arrive at the ocean knowing that this was always their destination.

You need not worry that by swimming with the current you will arrive at the sea too soon. The river mouth in this metaphor is not a fixed point. You reach the sea when you have exhausted your life force. By swimming with the current you move while conserving your energy.

Practice mindfulness

Being mindful in Nature in the way described in the *Every moment is the best moment* chapter allows the subtle complexities of Nature to reveal themselves to you and for those impressions to be received without being distorted through judgment and the superimposition of preconceived ideas. It is a common mental habit to receive a sense perception and straight away start processing it into various categories, working on it until the conclusion bears little resemblance to external reality.

Relax and merge

Many people in the developed world are tense and stressed. Our preoccupation with the drama of daily life creates a tension that over time becomes the baseline of our life. But look around in Nature, most of what you see is tranquil most of the time. Nature flows gently in quietly evolving cycles from one state to its opposite. Violent explosions of energy such as storms are the exception that proves the rule that Nature is tranquil most of the time.

Communing with Nature is releasing your worries and stress-producing thoughts, and, breathing deeply you synchronise your inner world with the slower, more relaxed rhythms of Nature in the here and now. Past and future do not exist in this mind-set, only the present.

You have achieved this state of merged presence when you are experiencing Nature in a fully conscious, non-conceptual way. It is heightened awareness without the mental chatter. You might recall this is the essence of meditation.

As you progress with this practice you become aware that in Nature there a vast moving river of intelligent energy all around you. This passage from Hermann Hesse's novel *Siddhartha*, illustrates the point beautifully:

However, amongst the thousands (of travellers wishing to cross the river) there have been a few, four or five, to whom the river was not an obstacle. They heard its voice and listened to it, and the river has become holy to them, as it has to me. The river has taught me to listen; you will learn from it too. The river knows everything; one can learn everything from it.

Unconditional love and compassion

Aligning your inner nature with the larger Nature outside and establishing this as a habit will bring with it an increasingly powerful feeling of unconditional love for all things. This is the essential quality of Nature as it nourishes all life.

As a natural consequence of the experience of unconditional love, you are likely to have an increasing desire to help others in the spirit of compassion. This might take the form of spontaneous acts of kindness, *'paying it forward'*, or other forms of self-less action. All of these are the result of allowing the outer reality of Nature to become your inner reality. You come to realise that the non-conceptual intelligence that pervades Nature manifests itself as intuition. What could be simpler, or more beautiful, than to build that bridge between inner and outer reality? This is a natural path towards cultivating an awareness of your highest self, and creating the right conditions for spontaneous Enlightenment.

Source awareness

As you increasingly dwell in a mind-set of unconditional love and compassion, you intuitively sense that you have reached the threshold of a great experience, that of pure Source awareness. No words can properly describe the blissful immersion of this experience. It is Enlightenment experienced as an ecstatic home-coming.

The Source is experienced as a formless clear light that you know was never born and will never die. In Tibetan Buddhism, the Source is poetically described as *the luminous splendour of the colourless light of emptiness*.

You realise that at your core you are this clear light, this beatific non-conceptual intelligence that permeates the entire universe. You don't just *think* it, you *experience* the knowing at a deep level. The recognition of this deep bond liberates you from the fear of death, permanently transforming the way you think about this most fearful aspect of life, the extinction of the egoic self. You become like a raindrop that falls into the ocean and becoming one with something immensely larger.

By summonsing the courage to leave what is left of your egoic self behind, and stepping across that experiential threshold you will have achieved Enlightenment. Now the challenge will be to maintain Enlightenment, or Source awareness and continue to dwell in an enlightened state despite the mundane world clamouring for attention.

7. Being rational

Rationality is a pre-eminent quality of high achieving people. While other creatures display some ability to reason, humans excel at it.

Being rational allows us to transcend our more primitive natures and make wise, informed choices. Rationality affords people the *power to choose* through an awareness of their options. Irrational people tend to act out earlier behaviour patterns without benefit of self-awareness and available choices.

Yet if we look at the spectrum of human thought and action in the world around us, it is clear that many people are operating from the more instinctive levels of mind; the pursuit of money, power and sex. They might be using logic to acquire what they desire, but the underlying motive is unconscious and unquestioned.

These folk still have the capacity think rationally in pursuit of the higher order needs of self-esteem and self-actualisation; they just do not exercise that choice.

Rationality & science

Modern science has been criticised for being too *empirical*, that is to say, too focussed on needing objective evidence before believing something. Indeed, hard-core rationalists can be frustrating with their dogged scepticism.

A more balanced view of the world is called for. There is a place for science and a place for intuitively-derived knowledge too. In an ideal world we would have them working together synergistically, balancing left brain rationality and right-brain creativity.

Yet science has brought so many benefits to human-kind. Not too long ago in the 1600's, the English philosopher Thomas Hobbes rightly observed that people's lives tended to be *solitary, poor, nasty, brutish and short*. In the meantime, science has greatly improved the quality and duration of human life generally. For that I am profoundly grateful every day; grateful for the diagnostic science that detected the same cancer in me that killed my mother, and the science that has kept my daughter alive.

So how does a scientifically-minded person reconcile themselves with being an Artful Traveller? By recognising that some if not most of the greatest scientific minds in history used intuition and imagination as the source of great ideas which they then applied empirical research methods to, turning intuition into 'good science'.

As Einstein said *imagination is more important than knowledge*. He and other giants from the world of science who have changed the world have observed that their best ideas have come from carefully honed Intuition. When Nils Bohr, a

contemporary of Einstein said that everything we call real is
made of things that cannot be regarded as real he was
expressing the paradox that cannot be explained by the
logical scientific mind, but which can be apprehended by the
intuitive mind. The truth is not only strange but stranger
than you can imagine.

On a personal level, I have had the privilege of working
with more than a few brilliant minds. The most brilliant was
Geoff Dromey, a professor of software engineering who
despite a formidable career was a humble man who
meditated daily and learned classical Greek so he could read
the original texts. When Geoff talked it was in a quiet voice,
but always worth listening to. He only talked when he had
something to say, not to be competitive. After he died, his
widow said meditation was the source of his most brilliant
ideas, the ones that made the biggest difference and earned
him fame. He never spoke of being a Zen practitioner; he
simply lived it every moment and let his actions speak for
themselves.

On the nature of Evil

To illustrate how science can help us resolve thorny
philosophical problems, at least to our own satisfaction,
consider the question of Evil. If we turn to religion, we
quickly lose ourselves in a labyrinth of abstractions that does
more to legitimise the religion itself than to answer the
question.

Neuro-science is helpful in seeing the nature of evil in a new light. The human brain is a work-in-progress that has evolved over hundreds of millions of years. Buried deep in the human brain are the same formations found in primitive reptilian brains. This is the *Limbic System*, and it contains elements such as the *Amygdala* (primitive impulses of pleasure, fear, and reproduction, amongst other things), and the *Hippocampus* (spatial memory, navigation). These formations are there because they work. Reptiles have been using them for a very long time, around 300 million years since they first emerged from the steaming swamps of the late Carboniferous period. What they do to survive is not evil because they do not know any better.

Evil is the label we put on some human behaviours that derive from this primitive brain but which we humans have the neural capacity to recognise as violent, aggressive, anti-social. With our higher consciousness we characterize some of the behaviours of the primitive brain as evil. In classifying it as morally wrong, we simultaneously create a class of moral good. Our mind becomes a moral battleground between our less evolved and more evolved selves.

We should accept and not judge ourselves for having a primitive side to our natures. It is an inextricable part of being human. Perhaps the purpose of evil is to give definition to the higher qualities of compassion, love, kindness, self-sacrifice. These would be meaningless without the contextual background of evil. The important thing is that we consciously identify with and choose to live through our higher self.

Science has removed guilt from the question of evil in this example. It is liberating to see oneself as a multi-layered being whose primitive side is capable of doing harm, but whose higher nature is capable of being a constructive force in the world. We consciously choose on a moment-by-moment basis. We accept that we may not always do the constructive thing. In a moment of weakness we might do harm. If that happens, we know to make proper amends and resolve to never repeat the act. Guilt need not take up residence in our minds and damage our self-esteem.

Evolutionary Psychology

Other branches of science that are helpful in understanding the nature of the human condition is Evolutionary Psychology and Anthropology.

Consider the human ego. Spiritual traditions are strongly in favour of finding ways to diminish one's ego with all of its competitiveness and attachment to people and things. Yet the majority of people in the world think that their ego is what defines them as a human being. 'I' am a person with a name, a life story.

Spiritual traditions like Buddhism make it clear that the ego is the greatest impediment to spiritual growth through its tendency to become attached. Being attached to any worldly thing always leads to suffering, since nothing in the world is permanent and any attachment to impermanence is certain to cause suffering. All worldly entities, like the egoic self, social structures, relationships, human lives and cultures are bound to pass away sooner or later. People in the unenlightened state naturally form attachments to these impermanent things, thus creating the foundation for suffering. The underlying cause of attachment is desire, which manifests in a multitude of ways; it can be desire for higher status, wealth, sexual gratification, popularity, food, comfort, more possessions of all kinds to name a few.

The enlightened person understands the mind's tendency to form attachments to worldly things, including, and perhaps most importantly, the concept of egoic self. They work daily to reduce this attachment, and recognise that while the objects of our desires were once life affirming goals that increased our chances of survival in a savage world back in humanity's evolutionary past, these days, in a civilised world of plenty these aspects of our more primitive self need to be eliminated if we are to progress.

The previous two paragraphs are straight from the second of Buddha's four noble truths (which was the first speech he made after becoming enlightened). Let us use science to make this profound message more understandable in the modern context.

Evolutionary Psychology tells us that the human ego is a survival mechanism that has evolved for our survival in a hostile environment, going back millions of years. The ego is very good at devising survival strategies. It categorizes what it encounters as either helpful or harmful to its survival. The ego creates a world of dualities, of polar opposites. It is quite understandable that there should be a part of our psyche that does this, given the on-going imperative to survive.

The ego is especially strengthened and defined by conflict. In the absence of conflict, it will create conflict in order to strengthen itself. The world is full of people whose lives consist of one conflict-driven drama after another. They are locked in egoic thinking, dancing to the war-drums that have been beating in the human psyche for hundreds of thousands of years.

But as the world becomes more civilised, and humanity evolves to a higher level of consciousness, we begin to see that having solved or eliminated most of the problems that threatened our ancestors, egoic thinking as a survival mechanism is no longer as helpful as it once was. Take for example our instinct to eat salty, fatty and/or sweet foods. It helped us survive to store energy in body fat and have it in reserve the next time food is scarce.

In our evolutionary past it was impossible to find so much salty/ fatty/ sweet food that it would harm you, so we are programmed to eat as much of it as we can find, as often as possible. In today's world though, we have to curb this tendency if we are not going to become obese. Our higher rational self needs to recognize that seeing the world through the eyes of our primitive ancestors, with danger in every rustling bush, is no longer helpful to our well-being.

Seven deadly sins

Another example of how our more primitive natures no longer serve us well is the *Seven Deadly Sins*. In Catholicism, these serve as a warning to avoid certain behaviours that might condemn a person's mortal soul to hell. These behaviours include being angry, greedy, lazy, proud, lustful, envious and gluttonous.

These behaviours have been deemed morally wrong in a civilised world, but consider how each of these behaviours would have improved our primitive ancestors' survival prospects:

Anger is an advantage as a warning to a potential attacker, or it acts as a stimulus to fight ferociously if necessary.

Greed makes a person acquire useful commodities like food, weapons, shelter, reproductive partners, animal skins, access to drinking water etc, all of which improves their survival chances.

Sloth or laziness conserves energy. Food was scarce in the Pleistocene with its repeated Ice Ages; people would have been cold and hungry if not starving for much of the time. Survival would have depended on conserving one's energy for the high-dividend activities like hunting or defence.

Pride enhances self-esteem. High self-esteem improves survivability because it leads an individual to value themselves and therefore be more likely to claim and fight for the resources they need to survive.

Lust is the desire to reproduce and pass on one's genetic material to the next generation.

Envy makes a person more likely to go after another's possessions on the assumption that if others value those things enough to obtain them in the first place, they must be worth having for oneself.

Gluttony takes advantage of abundant food while it lasts, laying down fat reserves to help an individual through the famine that was always just around the corner for the Pleistocene human.

Science helps us to understand how much of our behaviour derives from our primitive past without resorting to guilt. From this understanding, we are able to make a conscious, rational choice to refrain from behaving in these ways.

Some of our instincts still serve us well; for example the instinct to love and nurture our children. By being fully conscious, we can choose to continue behaviour that is helpful, and discontinue that which is unhelpful.

Understanding

Another evolutionary trait that gets in the way of harmonious experience is the tendency to rush to judgment.

It was important in the ancestral environment to rapidly assess a situation and take appropriate action. If you heard a rustle in the nearby bushes, it was wise not to think too long about it, wondering about the philosophical meaning of the sound. But in the civilised world where things are more complex than dangerous, it is more adaptive to suspend judgment at least long enough to properly understand a complex situation. Preferably one should suspend judgment altogether and remain open-minded.

Judgment and understanding are mutually exclusive. When you make a judgment about something, you declare the matter closed, no further consideration necessary. While you might have categorised the situation, you will be unable to understand any better than you already.

The Artful Traveller therefore keeps their mind open, sensing the reality around them directly rather than engaging in complex reasoning based on their existing prejudice.

Ethnocentric thinking

'There are no foreign lands. It is the Traveller only who is foreign.' – Robert Louis Stevenson.

People have an innate tendency to think that their own culture is the only truly valid one, and every other culture is less correct or somehow wrong. Like a fish swimming in the ocean, they are barely aware of the water, only noticing when it is gone, replaced by something else. In Anthropology this is called being *ethnocentric*.

People are like this because humans evolved in family groups, relying on each other for survival. One's family was the in-group, and by definition everyone else was an outsider and a potential enemy. This 'us and them' orientation worked for us on the savage savannah, but in the civilised world where there are rules for everything and everyone is connected to everyone else economically and in other ways, xenophobia works against our interests.

The xenophobic instinct has long been the basis of human conflict. It is a tough one to subdue. We probably inherited it from the common ancestor we share with our primate cousins. People look at their neighbour and see an enemy whose land and resources they want for themselves. Or we look at them and imagine they are getting ready to attack us to take our land, so we launch a pre-emptive attack.

As a remedy for xenophobia, we should recognise that despite the differences in physical appearance, religion and culture, all humans everywhere are so genetically similar as to be almost identical. We are the same species after all. Any man and any woman, regardless of where they are from could produce a child. It is a fact that we are all members of one, very large family. When we look at a stranger, we might use empathy to see the world through their eyes and doing so realise that we would probably think and act just like them if we were in their place. That stranger is no stranger, they are us and we are them.

Shakespeare makes the point in *Merchant of Venice*. This quote is spoken by Shylock, a Jew, though the sentiment is true for anyone:

Hath not a Jew eyes? Hath not a Jew hands, organs, dimensions, senses, affections, passions; fed with the same food, hurt with the same weapons, subject to the same diseases, heal'd by the same means, warm'd and cool'd by the same winter and summer as a Christian is? If you prick us, do we not bleed? If you tickle us, do we not laugh? If you poison us, do we not die? And if you wrong us, shall we not revenge? If we are like you in the rest, we will resemble you in that (Act III, scene I).

8. Airline etiquette

If the 20th Century saw the birth of air travel, the 21st Century is when low-cost air travel for the masses became a reality. It is faster and cheaper to travel to the other side of the world than ever before, and the trend is set to continue. But there is downside of travelling Economy/Coach class that is well-known to every traveller.

The flying Flâneur would have been a foreign concept to Baudelaire, but in the 21st Century the Artful Traveller has acquired a whole new set of indispensable skills. It is to know how to make the experience of budget air travel more tolerable if not enjoyable for themselves and their fellow travellers. The less psychological and physical stress that result from a flight, the better the state you will be in when you arrive.

The psychology of airline travel

There is something about air travel that brings out the worst in people. The phenomena has much to do with (a) *claustrophobia* leading to heightened anxiety, and (b) the perceived *invasion of personal space* leading to attempts to reclaim it.

Claustrophobia

Cramming strangers shoulder to shoulder, elbow to elbow into an aluminium tube for many hours, thinning the available oxygen so it is like being on a 4000 metre (10,000 feet) high mountain, then hurtling that tube through the sky at close to the speed of sound at an altitude of 10 kilometres (6 miles) are the ideal conditions for any sane person to experience some degree of claustrophobia.

Personal space (Proxemics)

Every one of us as we go through life maintains four concentric zones (like a bulls-eye target) around us; *Intimate* space (0 to 45 cm), *Personal* space (45 to 120cm), *Social* space (1.2 to 3.7 metres) and *Public* space (3.7 to 8 metres and beyond). These are average figures. Actual figures vary from culture to culture.

It is not difficult to see where the problem with airline travel arises, indeed with any form of public transport where we are crammed together with strangers. People we do not know belong in the public space (no closer than 3.7 metres or 12 feet away from us if we are to feel comfortable. Instead, these strangers are put into intimate (0 to 45 cm) contact with us as our shoulders and elbows unavoidably rub together.

Our instincts are telling us that this is a violation, while our rational minds try to keep our rising indignation under control. If we are not mindful though, our instincts assert themselves in a variety of ways and here is where the problems arise for the people around us.

All of these factors combine to create a sense of discomfort with our present situation and the desire to escape from it as soon as possible. Observe how most passengers stand up as soon as the plane comes to a rest at its destination, even though everyone knows it will be several minutes before anyone can actually get off the plane. The rational thing to do would be to stay seated and relaxed until it is possible to stand up and walk off.

An attitude of gratitude

Gratitude is an emotion that has enormous power, both in making a journey more pleasant and in life generally, but which few people understand in our consumer-driven world that encourages dissatisfaction and complaint.

What is there to be grateful for with economy air travel? Quite a lot actually. A hundred years ago, travelling several thousand kilometres would have been immensely arduous, time-consuming, uncomfortable and dangerous, not to mention expensive. How fortunate you are to be able to avoid all that for just a few hundred dollars and a couple of hours of your valuable time. Unless we figure out how to beam people from place to place like in Star Trek, it is still the easiest way to get to far-off places.

An attitude of gratitude will endear you to the airline staff. So accustomed are they to rude and demanding passengers that the ones who actually notice and appreciate them will be looked after. All you need do is to make brief eye contact, and with a friendly smile and a nod, say hello or thank you, depending on the situation. This not only makes them feel better about doing a difficult job, it makes you feel better too. It is a win-win situation.

Before the flight

Through a combination of *patience* and *consideration*, the boarding process can be accomplished without stress.

Patience

Patience in accepting that getting several hundred people seated and settled is always going to take at least 20 minutes. If you know it is inevitable and you have no control over the process, it is best to simply accept that it is so and not wish that it were otherwise.

Consideration

Consideration is not taking longer than is necessary to get yourself seated. I have often observed people holding up a long line of passengers as they take their sweet time putting their bags in the over-head locker, carefully folding their coat etc, apparently oblivious to the people waiting to get past. That is not being considerate. If possible, step aside from the aisle and stand in the foot-well of the aisle seat while you arrange your bits and pieces.

If someone is already sitting in the aisle seat and you need to get past them to the middle or window seat, make eye contact, and apologetically smile as you communicate your need for them to get up and let you past. It is important to make a good first impression on the people that you will be sharing a confined space with for the next so many hours.

If you are allocated to the aisle seat and there is no-one sitting next to you yet, be ready to get up and do so graciously. Try to not indulge in wishful thinking that those seats will remain unoccupied. They almost certainly will have someone allocated to them, they just haven't arrived yet.

It's a cell phone not a megaphone

People talking on cell phones often speak louder than they need to. Everyone within a ten meter radius can hear their side of the conversation.

When boarding and waiting for departure, be considerate to your fellow passengers by moderating the volume of your voice so that only the intended person at the other of the call can hear you.

This advice is applicable in almost every situation where a cell phone is used.

During the Flight

Contain yourself in your allocated space

As confined as the average economy/coach class seat is, endeavour to contain your arms, legs and girth between your armrests. While your neighbour may tolerate a minor encroachment into their space, deciding it not worth making a fuss over, they will certainly notice it and resent it to some degree. Never assume that people will not notice or mind encroachment on their already limited space.

The battle for the armrest

This is probably the most hotly contested zone of all. Economy class armrests are barely wide enough for one arm, so someone will always be the loser unless a way can be found to share the armrest. This can be accomplished by allowing your neighbour to have the armrest to themselves initially. Their arm will rest somewhere near the middle. After a half hour or so, gently insert your own arm onto the rear part of the armrest, the part closest to the seat-back. Do so unaggressively, gradually. The other person will usually shift their own arm forwards following the line of least resistance. By doing this you are sending the unspoken message that there is no good reason why you both cannot share the armrest, and that it is only reasonable to do so.

The best kind of neighbour simply lets the other have the armrest, particularly when that person is sitting in the middle seat. The worst kind assumes ownership of both armrests and refuses to share. Possession is nine tenths of the law in their selfish minds. These are often alpha individuals who assume they deserve the lion's share of the available resources and who probably regard travelling economy as an affront to their dignity.

What can you do about the space hog? Politely asserting your right to an equal share of the available space is the best policy. There is a fine line between being assertive and aggressive. Assertiveness comes from a place of respect for others and the reasonable demand that others afford you the same respect.

Aggressiveness rides rough-shod over the rights of others, and unless you enjoy being bullied, you will feel better about yourself if you show the bully that their actions will not be tolerated. This is usually enough to get them to back down. In extreme cases where open conflict occurs, the cabin crew will get involved, but you really do not want the situation to come to this. There is a good chance both of you will be blamed equally for the disturbance. Creating a disturbance on a flight is enough to get you banned from flying with that airline in the future, even criminal charges.

The rapid recliner

After armrests, the reclined seat-back is the next most contentious zone of potential conflict. The worst thing a passenger can do is suddenly recline their seat all the way back without regard for what impact this will have on the person behind. They may have their tray table down, with food, bottles, their laptop computer, and all kinds of things on there, and the rapid recliner sends all of this crashing.

Sure, you have a right to recline your seat, no-one is disputing that, but it must be done in such a way that shows consideration for the person behind. That means to recline SLOWLY. If you do it gradually and in two stages, the person behind will barely notice. The first stage is to take it slowly to half way. The second stage, done perhaps half an hour later, goes all the back, again slowly.

It is not uncommon for an aggrieved person sitting behind to randomly kick the seat in front. If you are being kicked, and it is not a child doing it, there is a fair chance this is why. Understand that you might have contributed to the situation.

Under your seat

There is a misconception that the space under your seat belongs to you; it does not. If you try to put your cabin luggage under your seat, you are likely to be indignantly told to move it by the passenger behind whose foot room has been suddenly diminished.

At 180cm (6′) I am not especially tall, yet even I find that my feet reach all the way under the seat in front. When something gets shoved into that space by the person in front, I slowly push it forwards into their own foot-space. As long as your feet do not project any further than the vertical boundary of the front edge of the seat in front, you are within your own space.

Getting up

A considerate passenger sitting either in the middle or window seat will minimise how many times they expect the aisle seat person to get up and down to let them in and out. Often the best way is to wait for the aisle-set passenger to get up to go to the toilet or stretch their legs, and do the same yourself. They will probably realise that you have considerately waited for them. If they are already seated when you return, they only need get up the once, not twice. They will also know that you will be back soon, and will not settle down until you do. All of this sends a message that you are considerate neighbour and earns you a certain amount of good-will credit.

When getting up, the natural thing to do is to grab the top of seat back of the row in front and use it to leverage yourself out. If you do this, do so carefully to minimise how much you move the seat back. The passenger in that seat might be trying to sleep. In any event, they will consider it an intrusion to have their seat shaken.

On long, over-night flights, when most of the aircraft is asleep, you might find yourself unable to sleep and wanting to stretch your legs and perhaps go to the toilet. But to do so will involve either waking the aisle-seat passenger up or asking them to move, something they will definitely resent having to do, or climbing over them without making any contact at all. Unless you are agile enough to do this, resign yourself to staying put, or trying again to get some sleep. The thin, dehydrated air that you have been breathing for hours will have decreased the likelihood that you need to go to the toilet unless you have been drinking alcohol.

If you know you have a small bladder and need to go to the toilet frequently, request an aisle seat. If you in the aisle seat and the person nearer the window needs to frequently go, suggest you swap seats.

The window shade

Airlines generally require that window shades be fully open for take off and landing. What happens in between is at the discretion of the window seat passenger. Open or close the shades as appropriate to the circumstances and having done so, leave it alone. Do not keep opening and closing it.

If the flight is an over-nighter and people expect to sleep, the cabin crew will ask the window seat passengers to close the shades on the side of the plane that the rising sun will shine on so that people will not be dazzled by high intensity sun-beams.

Moderate how much alcohol you consume

The thin, dry air of modern aircraft has a dehydrating effect on passengers so drinking enough fluids to stay hydrated is important. Bear in mind that alcohol is a diuretic, something that makes your body excrete more water than it otherwise would, so there is a strong possibility that drinking too much alcohol on a flight will cause you to become dehydrated. This is why the flight attendants bring around water every so often.

The airlines walk a fine line with regards to alcohol on flights. Give people enough alcohol and they will drift off into a pleasant slumber and be no trouble at all. Give them too much and they can become drunk and disorderly, abusing their fellow passengers and generally being a problem.

The cabin crew will not serve alcohol to a person who is visibly drunk. So if you want to keep drinking, you *must* remain calm and composed, the kind of person who can hold their drink. On an over-night flight, you could walk down to the kitchen and politely ask for a stiff night-cap to help you get to sleep. Flight attendants like it when the passengers sleep and who could blame them?

Kicking children, screaming babies

What to do when the child behind is kicking your seat? The worst thing you can do is over-react. It makes you look like you are being mean to a sweet little kid. The best course of action is to stay calm, and get ready to have a quiet word with the person who is in charge of the child. Do not speak directly to the child.

When ready, turn to the carer, smile and say hello. Assure them by your demeanour that you are not angry and pose no threat. Control your anger before attempting this. All of this has the effect of not raising defences that are easily raised when children are concerned.

Say something like *I know it is difficult for kids to sit still on flights, but the kicking is really disturbing me. Is there some way you can get him/her to stop? Anything you can do would be greatly appreciated.*

Doing this makes you seem kindly and reasonable. Unless the carer is negligent, they will readily see your point and do what they can to stop it.

If that fails, you could always try having a quiet word with the flight attendant. Use a variant of the same speech.

Crying babies are a different matter. Most of the time, there is nothing you can do except wait for the poor little thing to settle down of their own accord.

Follow the flight attendant's directives

It is worth remembering that the flight attendants act under the legal authority of the Captain. When they give you a directive, like returning to your seat, you are legally obliged to do what they say because it is actually Captain saying it.

Defying the Captain's authority is a criminal offence (a felony). In the post-911 world, there is close to zero tolerance for passengers making a nuisance of themselves on aeroplanes.

Hitting or shoving a member of the crew or another passenger is a serious criminal matter that is certain to result in you being arrested on arrival and charged with a felony that could result in a hefty fine and/or serious jail time, even if such behaviour is normal at your local bar or pub on a Friday night. In the US, if this is Strike 3, the consequences are very serious indeed.

The talkative passenger

It is a fact of human nature that extroverts like to talk while introverts prefer to stay silent. When you put either kind into an aeroplane for hours, their natural tendencies seem to be magnified. The talkative person becomes more talkative, the introspective person becomes more introspective. This is probably a response to the heightened anxieties of airline travel.

As a general rule, do not assume your neighbour wants to chat, particularly when it might go on for hours and hours. Assume they want their privacy and only start a conversation if it is clear that is what both of you want.

If you happen to be in a chatty mood, wait until the plane is about half and hour from landing and strike up a conversation then. If it has been a long flight, your neighbour is likely to welcome some light conversation when there is no chance of being trapped in it for hours.

The mile-high club

Sex between consenting adults is of course not a crime unless it happens within the sight of others. Sex in an aeroplane toilet or under a blanket in your seat technically comes under the category of being a public place, so it is illegal if not uncomfortable. Certainly the airline would prefer that you did not do it. However provided you are discrete and do not cause a problem for others, it is a matter between you and your consenting adult partner.

Personal hygiene

It hardly needs to be said that doing everything you can to minimise personal odour, including not wearing too much perfume or after-shave, is a basic requirement for people travelling together in a tightly packed, hermetically sealed environment. Freshly washed body and clothes are the obvious starting point.

Acceptable levels of body odour are culturally-defined. What is considered acceptable in the developing world might be unacceptable in North America or Europe.

After the Flight

Stay seated until it is possible to disembark

Most passengers stand up as soon as the plane comes to a rest, even though they know it will be several minutes before they can actually leave. Stay seated and relaxed until it is possible to stand up and walk off.

Double check you have the right bag

After claiming your bag from the carousel, double-check that it is really your bag. Imagine the inconvenience of getting to your hotel and discovering the truth. Imagine how

much bother you are causing the bag's real owner. Easily
avoided by a quick check before leaving the baggage
collection area.

Appendix A: Meditation made simple

Many readers of this book will already be practicing meditation, and need no further encouragement to do this most beneficial of activities. If you already have a meditation regime, or would like to improve on what you are already doing, or if you do not meditate at all, this chapter outlines the distilled essence of meditation practice.

Once you know the essential basics, you can adapt the technique to suit your needs. Meditation is something that can be learned in a few minutes, but which can take a lifetime to perfect. *The greater the truth, the more simply it can be expressed.* Think of Einstein's $E=mc^2$ equation (the energy contained in an object equals the mass of the object multiplied by the square of the speed of light). This is a great, fundamental truth that has been expressed very simply which gives it great impact. Einstein could have said it in 100,000 words and the statement would be just as true, but the impact would be far less because so many people would not have penetrated to the heart of this truth.

Meditation establishes primary attention on your inner self where it should be. It allows you to shift your attention away from the clamouring demands of a complex outer world with its strident messages and competing demands. When you meditate every day, you can continue to live in the material world, but that world is placed into its proper perspective as your secondary reality.

Meditation creates a peaceful inner space within which you can become aware of the more subtle aspects of yourself that have been hitherto obscured by the noise of the outer world. In this space, your intuition grows stronger, revealing to you a rich stream of subtle but powerful knowledge to help you germinate the seeds of enlightenment that lie ready in you. Meditation is free and completely natural.

Simple method for meditation

Meditation is heightened awareness without the mental chatter.

With our restless minds in control and demanding entertainment, it may seem that meditation is difficult. Plus there are so many approaches a person can take. It is good to know that there is a very simple and effective method that anyone can use, almost anytime they want. It is the essence of every meditation method, and is so simple that it only takes a few minutes to learn, though longer to master.

Begin by sitting comfortably and begin to breathe rhythmically. Sit with spine straight but in a way that will not induce sleep. Breathe deeply, from the diaphragm, in through your nose and out through your mouth. Breathing is really the key here. The fresh oxygen that enters your bloodstream has an almost immediate, beneficial effect, inducing a sense of well-being. But be careful of your posture. If you are too comfortable sleep will not be far away.

Sleep is definitely not meditation. Sleep is unconsciousness, not heightened consciousness.

Focus your conscious awareness on the place immediately behind the centre of your forehead, the so-called third eye. This is the place that mystics believe is the seat of the soul, or highest self. Imagine that in this place there is a crystal about the size of a marble. There is a whole universe contained in that crystal, a perfect, scaled-down copy of the larger universe. Feel the crystal warming up, beginning to glow. The glow becomes a powerful beacon of light, radiating out in all directions, getting brighter and stronger, bathing your body and everything around you with pure loving energy. Your highest self is doing this. You have a powerful desire to bring your highest self into your everyday awareness.

After centring your awareness and then allowing it to expand outwards, continue to consciously **breathe deeply and rhythmically**. Concentrate your awareness on the in-breath without engaging in any mental commentary. Simply be aware of the breath as it comes in, and be likewise aware as it goes out, all the while remaining centred, aware and thoughtless. This rhythmic breathing and focussed awareness is the essence of meditation. Practicing this alone will give you as much benefit as the many courses offered by new age organisations.

You can **count sub-vocally on the out-breath** up to a certain number of breaths, (say 50). Or you can set a timer to remind you when ten minutes has passed. Ten minutes is a good duration to begin with. Do the ten minutes for two weeks or so until it becomes well-established, then gradually increase the duration up to 30 minutes over the weeks that follow.

Your goal should be to **meditate in this way for up to 30 minutes, twice a day.** It is good to begin your day with a meditation session. Likewise end the day with a session in the evening not long before bed-time.

Of course, as you get used to your meditation practice, and start to feel the benefits (stress reduction, more even-tempered, expanded awareness, intuitive insights, increased creativity, improved relationships, enjoyment of life, to name a few) you may feel inclined to take some time during the day to meditate, say at lunch time. Just choose a safe place where you won't be disturbed for half an hour, if that is possible. Even if it is not, you can snatch a few minutes here and there and still derive worthwhile benefit.

How do you know if you are doing it right? Remember, meditation is heightened awareness without the mental chatter. If you can get yourself into a state of heightened awareness and are able to quiet your mind of the chatter for a period of time, then you are meditating. By doing this, you switch off the ego, activate the part of the brain where higher awareness lives, and flush your body with plenty of oxygen. It will make you feel relaxed with a deep sense of well-being.

Meditating for a short time is not difficult. Doing it for 15 or 20 minutes twice a day for the rest of your life will be more challenging. Resolve to meditate regularly for two weeks. Fourteen days, that is not too much to commit to. At the end of this time, you should be feeling the benefits for yourself at a deep level, and this might be enough to establish meditation as a permanent part of your life.

Practice non-attachment

One of the hardest things about meditation is an undisciplined mind that insists on being listened to and entertained. A mind that generates random thoughts about all manner of things, a mind which jumps from one thought to another like a grasshopper. This describes most people, most of the time.

No matter how interesting or important or disturbing these thoughts might be, when meditating it is important that you do not allow your attention to latch onto these random thoughts. Imagine that they are like loose pages of a newspaper blowing in the wind. Allow the wind to carry the newspaper away and give them no further thought. Resist the impulse to catch the page and read the worldly news written upon it. Understand that all such news is short-lived and ultimately without any real substance. In other words, practice what Zen Masters would call non-attachment. Attachment to worldly things is a major cause of human suffering, since nothing in the world is permanent. That which we are attached to must soon change or disappear, and we suffer because what we were attached to is now gone. Practicing non-attachment removes the cause of suffering. Another way to look at this is to practice having very low expectations. With low expectations you will seldom if ever be disappointed. Non-attachment is the key to meditation. It is also the key to a contented, if not happy life in general.

Optional Mantra

Some meditation schools suggest you should recite a sacred mantra while meditating. It isn't strictly necessary, though. The simple method outlined above alone will have strongly focussing effect on the mind. If you want to use a mantra, you might use *Highest Self* (on the in-breath), *Awake!* (on the out-breath).

By addressing your own Highest Self, also known as the God Within, and bringing it to your consciousness, your egoic self begins to dissolve and you start to experience a sense of one-ness, or unity consciousness. In this state you become increasingly aware of the connectedness of all things that is the foundation of the Satori experience.

Being detached from your mind by becoming the observer of it activates in you a new dimension of thought. There is the 'I' that thinks your various thoughts, and then there is the awareness that watches the 'I' thinking those thoughts. That observer entity is an aspect of your Highest Self. Neuroscientists have observed on brain activity imaging devices that a person who is actively using this higher faculty is using one of the most recently evolved parts of the human brain.

Appendix B: About cameras

What is the right camera for the Artful Traveller? Many readers of this book will be experienced photographers who know cameras and need no advice on the matter. For everyone else, here is some general advice.

In keeping with Moore's Law, the quality of digital photography is improving rapidly, while the cost is falling. For the Artful Traveller, there are several requirements that will always be true.

Look for a user friendly camera with intuitive controls. They allow the Artful Traveller to become *one with it*. The camera feels like an extension of oneself. You come to know it intimately and can get it to do what you want without having to puzzle over it. Getting to know a camera in this way takes time and practice.

The camera should also come with a good lens, the best one you can afford. It should be able to take close-up macro shots, all the way up to telephoto. An 80mm zoom lens is about right. This gives you the maximum flexibility to compose shots, even at a considerable distance. You can take a close-up of a flower or a jewel in one shot, then immediately take a zoomed in shot of a far-off mountain or cathedral on a hill-top five kilometres away.

If a manufacturer has put a really good lens on a camera, they will also have made the rest of the camera good enough to do justice to the lens.

The Artful Traveller will also appreciate a camera that is compact and does not draw attention to itself. When not in use, it should be discretely out of sight. Nothing says tourist like a heavy camera bag full of expensive gear. In the eyes of the locals, this might seem like flaunting one's wealth.

Most digital cameras are also capable of high definition video thus removing the need to bring along a separate video camera on your travels.

The End

Printed in Great Britain
by Amazon.co.uk, Ltd.,
Marston Gate.